TWICE HOOKED

David Barr

Berkswell
1990

Line drawings by Rosa Pearson
The photographs (unless marked to the contrary)
are the property of the author

First published in 1990 by Berkswell Publishing Co Ltd
Warminster, Wiltshire.

ISBN 0 904631 07 09

Produced by John Stidolph
Typeset by Footnote Graphics, Warminster
Originated by NM Reproductions, Midsomer Norton
Printed by Bookcraft (Bath) Ltd.

Other books by David Barr

A Family Way
The Haig Guide to Salmon Fishing in Scotland
The Haig Guide to Trout Fishing in Britain

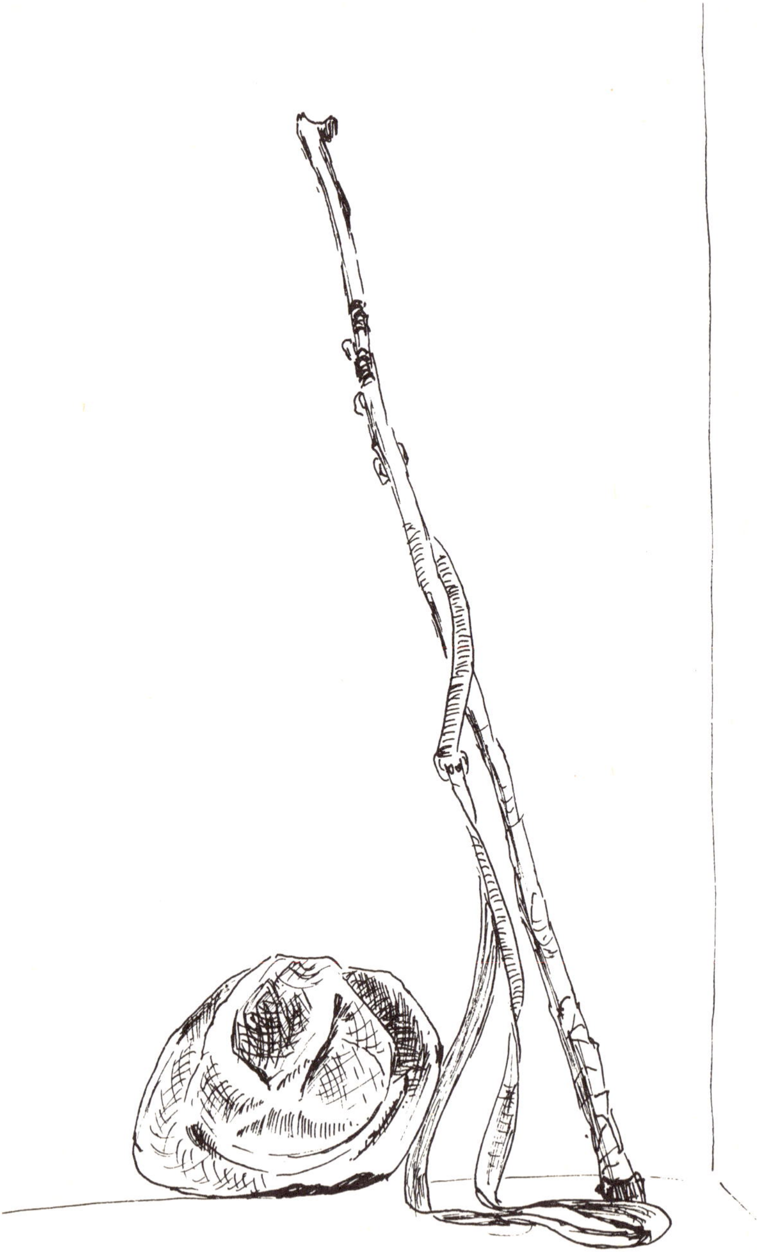

CHAPTER ONE

The Soldier's Dream

For four years and six months they kept me away from 'England, Home and Beauty' (which is how we sadly referred to the place). No country except our own sent its soldiers away for such a period. A six year prison sentence, with remission, is less long and does not have the danger. For me, it was my twenty-third to twenty-sixth years, all gone beyond recall and not a thing to be done about it. There were times when the impossibility of getting home made me feel claustrophobic, frustrated beyond endurance; but even if one had the nerve and the genuine inclination, deserting in the Middle East was not an alternative. There were consolations, of course, the main ones being the daily, weekly and monthly feat of having survived. To these were added spells in the Canal Zone, where irrigation made life greener, and leaves in Cairo, where the shops brimmed with good things like Dunhill pipes and Rolex Oysters and where even a trooper's pay (£1.50 a week accumulated whilst in the desert) opened the doors to quite good eating places and bars – but did not make available any of the local non-professional girls who were strictly classified as 'officers' only'. Most of all I was fortunate enough to sustain, early on, an injury that kept me away from the worst of the danger. The odds against a fighting soldier surviving four and a half years without being killed, severely wounded or captured, were no better than evens. My head injury was a blessing and I was lucky to have been singled out for it. When the brain began to clear, I found that I had been moved from the area of Tobruk to a base hospital that seemed like Eden.

As I walked from the ambulance to the tented ward a nursing sister muttered to her friend, 'Oh, poor boy'. It was lovely, a tiny bit of a hero at last. I realised that seven days had gone by and that I was wearing a beard on my juvenile features that might have affected a tender heart. While in this hospital I heard that in the next attack most of my squadron had been killed. Going back to the unit, or what was left of it, became even less attractive and (though I made the prescribed noises of frustration and disappointment) I was not sad when after some weeks in a convalescent camp in Palestine I was downgraded to B. That, fortunately, was a fairly honourable path away from the battles, because people with skull injuries did not thrive in 100° heat.

At that time I was a lance-corporal. Months passed, years passed, and I was playing cricket in Cairo. Some revered staff colonel spotted my talent with leg-breaks (who but a gentleman bowls leg breaks?), found out my name and number, and without informing me of his intentions or even exchanging the time of day (it was something that did not happen between colonels and lance-corporals), put in a report in which I was described as a 'born leader'. My own view was that, as a leader, I was in the mould of the Duke of Plaza Toro. I was despatched to a tented selection unit near Ismailia, where I won the game of bluff and double bluff they played at those places, and passed with honour. I had already decided that I would like to be an officer, if only to get after those forbidden Greek, Syrian, Jewish and Egyptian girls. Once again the machine took over and took me to Acre, the Middle East OCTU, from which I eventually emerged as a second lieutenant. There were still two years to go before my four and a half years were up – two years in which I was able to prove how much easier it had become to progress upwards. It had taken me nearly three years, from that awful night when I found myself in civilian clothes at Bovington camp, to get paid as a lance-corporal. Only two years later I had sprung from that to a few back-dated weeks paid as a lieutenant colonel. The letter from the Secretary of State for War, framed on our downstairs lavatory wall, tells me that, if I wish, which I do not, I could use the rank of Major – because the War Office tends to recognise the next highest rank.

I cannot pretend that being deprived of feminine company was the ultimate hardship, urgent and desirable as that company at times seemed. My real deprivation was, trifling as it may appear, of the opportunity to go fishing and to get to the places where fish live and may be caught.

I first took rod to river when I was about six and since then hardly a week passed when I was not fishing or preparing to – in pond, ditch, lake and river. Even during the interminable periods of imprisonment at boarding school I had found ways and means of keeping my hand in, and of maintaining a high degree of obsession. I even, brashly, took a fishing rod with me when I was called-up, and the horror of going to a tank training unit (instead of something more peaceful like the Pay Corps) was compensated for by the fishing I soon found to be available near Bovington. The River Frome flowed within a mile of the camp; in those days one did not ask for permission. On a night operation (when my NCO had allowed me to bring a rod in return for the catch) I wormed out three trout over two pounds from a very handy pool. I was not much good at the military arts, it was agreed, but as a fisherman I was unsurpassed. During the days in the desert, while the comrades shut their eyes and thought of beer (the drinking water was slightly saline which was no help to a thirst), I shut mine and pictured the brown glides of the Barle or the chalk-stream clarity of the Mill Brook at Blewbury, or even the weedy smells of some of the Thames weir pools (described by H. T. Sheringham as 'the odour of sanctity'). Old desert warriors in the Cairo cafés, incidentally, would display their experience by asking for a few grains of salt in their drinking water.

Just as there was no fishing, so too, equally doomed was

one's home love life. What sweet and lovely twenty-year-old was going to wait for the boyfriend who had vanished into the Middle East for four and a half years? We used to get frantic as the letters came in. For the bachelors it was the excuse for a steady period of drunkenness, for the married men the misery was compounded by all kinds of communications with welfare services, when married allowances were stopped and bitterness rose to explosive levels. It was not helped by unreliable airmail posts, and seamail letters that took seven weeks if they arrived at all. To the credit of one loving couple, a break-up of such unparallelled dimensions was contrived – with children being dismissed to welfare facilities all over the UK – that the Middle East Headquarters finally sent the husband home. (No one ever discovered how rapturous the reunion, how marvellous that triumph over the administrative generals.) Believe it or not the top organisation in Cairo was called O.2.E. At that one moment O.2.E. took a nice little slap in the face. Those not so clever became more and more convinced that the Poles and the Yanks were taking all the worthwhile women. Little but damaged goods would be left for us. A fairly nasty artillery captain was heard to observe on D. Day, 'There'll be lots of lovely widows for us now'. He didn't survive to get his.

Going home on a troop ship filled with those who had also put in their four and a half years, every man and every woman a hardened soldier, was a stimulating experience. Of discipline there was little sign. My one night as Orderly Officer was a laugh a minute. My best moments were on the top deck one evening, with members of the Everton Supporters' Club (they had them in those days and each one of us on that boat deck was a highly potential hooligan). We had a quiz on the names of the grounds of other league clubs and I came out on top (even though I was, as they reminded me, a f . . . . . . officer) when in the final round I named Elm Park as the home of Reading Football Club. I had imagined many times my return to that particular favourite haunt.

I am no longer certain where we landed – it was probably at Plymouth. There was a crowded train journey – then we were launched into a strange and unwelcoming London. Why ever should there have been a welcome? People were coming back – as well as going – all the time. Coming back was not much of a triumph – we were just lucky survivors, not dead, not maimed. We moved into the throngs of people, almost all in uniform, celebrating the fact that it was V.E. Day. Most people, men and women, were in uniform, the rest in the rather shabby formal clothes the war had left them. The atmosphere was like a return along Wembley Way after an English win – when there seemed no other means of celebrating than to jump and hug and sing. All the nation was having a fantastic party – but the nation knew each other. No one knew the passengers from the Middle East. I had lost touch with every one of my female contacts – and on V.E. Day and after four and a half years, one wanted more than female contacts. I wandered around with the singing hordes – attempting to sing songs I had never heard before. One or two tentative approaches to passing young women were staunchly rebuffed. I ended up in a single bed in some military-type club and put in a 'phone call to my mother in Hampshire. The next morning I was on my way to Winchester, the Test, the Dever, the Itchen and some girlfriends – or widows – in that order. This was what I had really come back for. Elm Park would not be open for two months.

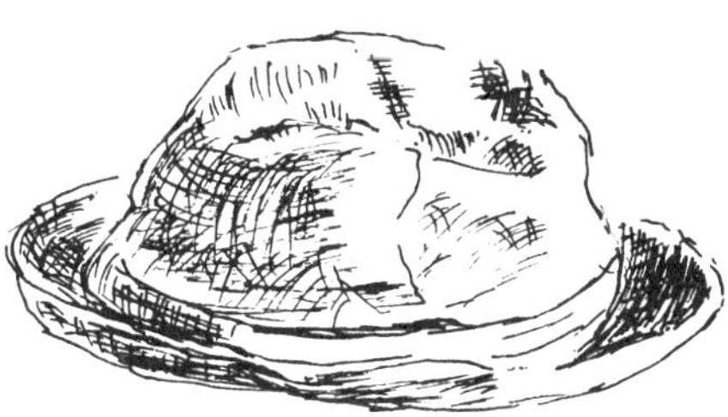

CHAPTER TWO

Fishing for the Forces

One soon grew chips on one's shoulders. There was no special welcome for returning heroes, nor for returning non-heroes. Moans were met with a quick, 'Don't you know there's a war on?' Everyone had moved. All the old haunts had changed or vanished. I began to feel more and more like a non-person until I stopped feeling sorry for myself and plunged into the marvellous variety of fishing that I suddenly discovered was available.

Someone (I hope he got a knighthood) had organised Fishing for the Forces. It was a scheme taken up by fishery proprietors with a zest that has never been seen before or since. But first there came the miracle of my fishing tackle. Heaven alone knows how many times my family had moved during the war – four or five for sure – leaving behind them all my books, all my precious 78 rpm records of Harry Roy, nearly all my clothes – but somehow, still in its faded case was my twenty first birthday present, a nine-foot Hardy Perfection split-cane fly rod (including the spare joint; it had not grown; it was still three inches shorter where I had broken it many years before). Nothing had warped either (the rods they made in those days were every bit as good as the rods that modern materials make possible). My St. George reel (in use today) was in need of nothing but a drop of oil; the Kingfisher silk line, though showing signs of battle fatigue, needed only to be annointed with floatant; a little polish on the ferrules and we were ready.

Within twenty four hours of registering, I had been invited

to two days on the Test, upstream of Stockbridge. I booked myself into the Grosvenor and walked across to Mr. Lunn's shop. I stocked up with dry flies that I had never dreamed of having a chance to use – Iron Blue Duns, Ginger Quills, Lunn's Particulars (of course), Houghton Rubies and, on special recommendation, Caperers. I even had a respectable landing net, which is more than I have now. By 10.30 that morning I was in a fishing paradise, welcomed by the owner (did I really detect a halo glistening above his head?) and succoured by the keeper. It was lucky about the succour because what little I had ever known about dry fly fishing I had forgotten, but not, luckily, about casting. My first practice cast flew out as if I had been doing it daily for years. The keeper nodded and wandered away leaving me to enjoy my day in solitude. Some of his forces guests had arrived with sixteen-foot poles, worms and floats.

On that first day on the Test it was inevitable that the sun would shine gently, with friendly cloud cover, just sufficient to prevent glare. Nothing could have upset the harmony of water birds, kingcups, and wild irises. Beautiful insects hovered and dived. This was worth winning any war for. I wondered, in case any eyes were on me, if I ought to go through the motions of gently dragging from the surface the mass of floating detritus, to identify the bodies of dead flies, even though I would not have been able to tell a dead dun from an upright. Then, in that moment of doubt, there was a splosh and a suck twenty yards ahead of me, followed by a widening gleaming circle. My rod was up; all I had to do was select the right fly. Because it looked the juiciest (the wrongest of reasons) I tied on the Caperer, touched it with mucillin, and with heart thumping like a water pump, waited, but not for long. In exactly the same place, another ravenous rise, the water bulging from the movement of a large fish body. I crept nearer, uttered a dozen propitiatory messages to any non-terrestrial being who would listen, started to lengthen my line and swish ... The non-terrestrial being had been listening. Two feet of gut cast (no nylon in those days – but mine had been soaking for ten minutes), headed by the Caperer, landed beyond the fish's lie. The fly floated cheekily downstream, the nose came out – and what a nose! – the sucking noise was repeated, I struck and wonder of wonders, hooked it. Three or four hectic minutes later it was lying in my landing net, a brilliant beauty, the biggest, loveliest trout – two pounds three ounces – that I had ever legitimately caught on fly. It was keepable and I had been told to catch two. So I killed it, taking it back to my sainted parent that night. The whole sequence was one I have savoured ever since.

The rest of my adventure on this super beat could never keep pace with such a start, though it was none the worse for that. I caught one more fish that weighed about two pounds and several of about a pound. After a lifetime of regarding pound trout as monsters I put these back with pleasure and a feeling of new-found sophistication. I also made my first acquaintance with grayling – the sight of which drew groans from the keeper. They were graceful fish whose huge dorsal fins gave them, when hooked, a deceptive feeling of size; though none of the ones I caught weighed more than three quarters of a pound. I slipped them back when no one was looking. (Higher authority thought the river would be well rid of them.) Their little rises continually deceived me – just the kind that a slyly feeding three and a half pound trout might make. Nor were they simple to catch – they rose more swiftly than the brown trout. The languid relaxed strike that I was developing was far too slow. I missed many of them, making me keener than ever to solve the mysteries of their feeding. Needless to say, in this wonderland, the sun continued to shine all the time, while breezes gently ruffled the surface.

The lesson I learned most thoroughly was that trout – the relatively unsophisticated trout that lived in the Test even in those days – are very selective feeders. I had one lovely hour, in particular, of real fishing. Ignorant though I was of many of the ways of a dry fly fisherman, my casting skills stood me in very good part. Consequently when I saw a most tempting rise on the far bank it could be handled with competence. With the angle necessary to cast from below the fish, I was involved in quite a long diagonal. 'They're taking Caperers well', I told myself and covered him, with great care, four times. Four times the fly was ignored – but just after the fourth pass it came up confidently and took something I couldn't see. I put on a small Lunn's Particular – same result. The fish kept rising, but not to me.

There are moments when it is not only vital to keep a strong nerve, but also to be able to see what the fish are taking and where – (at that time my eyesight was as good as could be hoped for; nowadays long distance glasses have become necessary) – because the one thing guaranteed to put a fish down is to strike when it takes a natural fly at the same instant as the Lunn's Particular floats by, a foot away.

It took time, care and quite a little apprehension, and the Ginger Quill and the Iron Blue Dun that followed were all ignored. I began to wish that I had one of the little butterfly nets that the Houghton Club members are said to use – from which identification of the fly on the water is made. My ignorance of entymology made this impossible – and by the time I had worked my way round to the Houghton Ruby I was beginning, in soccer parlance, to drop my head; but the arrival of this tiny, dainty white-winged fly was greeted with an immediate take. My trophy weighed just over two pounds, and had made the beginnings of a fisherman of me.

Those were two never-to-be-forgotten days. I only wish I could remember the name of the beat with certainty. I suspect it was Leckhampton. Anyway I disobeyed orders and gave the keeper a present (members of the forces on full pay and leave allowances were comparatively wealthy) and wrote to the haloed owner the most delighted of thank-you letters. I am afraid he may have moved by now, to his stew pond in the sky.

One of the wonders of that time, looking back, was the Test's beautiful condition. It surged along, clear and clean. Not a gallon could have been abstracted. The weeds waved in marvellous health. The insect life thrived. The banks were immaculate, as were all the sluices and works that contain and control the energies of such a river. The reason, I believe, was that the water bailiffs at the outbreak of war had, in the main, been elderly men who were able to continue, undisturbed, their work of genuine national importance. The sad thing is that the Test today is a deteriorating river, affected by chemicals and abstraction, and often clouded by algae. How the rich and powerful who own it have allowed this paradise to have become sullied, is beyond me.

CHAPTER THREE

Learning about Trout

Before I discovered salmon and seatrout, trout were the absolutely supreme excitement. They were also rare and difficult to find. When you found some, there were usually gamekeepers whose attitudes were always negative.

The family had moved to Blewbury in Berkshire. My mother never settled for any length of time in any house or area for more than a few years, but at Blewbury we managed nearly seven. It was, and is, a lovely little village, full of classic thatched cottages and even thatched walls.

I was six or seven and already fishing hard. One day I discovered that among the shoals of roach in the Mill Brook there were these occasional monstrous trout. It had taken a lot of persuasion to be allowed to go down to the stream on my own. Usually I had to be accompanied by a bored young woman from the house or a tolerant sister. The first free day was like a new life. I had a three-jointed rod, which cost 4/6d at the fishing tackle shop at Wallingford and was strong enough to pull out anything; my size 12 hooks were firmly attached, by the makers, to gut. Bait was normally dough and I became as adept as anyone at the gentle cast that floated downstream and did not disturb the shoal. The trout (I never found out from where they had escaped) were big – monstrous to my eyes. You could watch them in the clear water, motionless and close to the chalky bottom, every spot temptingly visible; but when a worm was delivered anywhere near one of them there was a puff of mud and the fish had vanished. Some of them were so big that as they went, a wave accompanied them up the stream. I spent a whole summer fruitlessly trying to catch them and only at the very end found out that if I left my bait in their lie, abandoned it and the rod, and came back in an hour's time, the trout had either swallowed the hook and bled to death or had broken the gut and vanished. When an account is being taken of some of the fouler things I have done, those efforts are going to rank high, though my counsel may, in mitigation, plead extreme youth.

At nine came a great adventure. I was sent away during an Easter holiday to Dulverton to fish the Barle. The services of the delightful Fred Tout had been engaged and a place reserved for me at the Green Hotel. A model T Ford met me at Dulverton Station and took me to the hotel. I had been given half-a-crown for its cost and the tip. I must have appeared to the proprietors like a scruffy little Lord Fauntleroy, arriving in my grey flannel suit and carrying my Hardy fly rod. I was even given a small corner table all of my own, with the daughter of the house (one of the early lady point-to-point riders) as my guardian angel. She pandered to my fascination with her beautifully patted balls of butter, by doubling my supply, thus earning my undying affection.

Mr Tout, with total patience, patrolled the Barle with me, three hours a day for six days. He probably did not charge even a quarter of his real worth, because the family finances were dangerously stretched. Those were the days when first comments on new friends were not on intelligence or wit, but richness or poorness. We certainly were 'poo-er'; that is how it was pronounced.

Thanks to Mr Tout, my casting got better and better until I was throwing a line (to the rhythm of his 'one . . . two') right across that huge river. I went and had a day's fishing there after the war and was amazed at how it had shrunk.

The Barle trout were highly unco-operative – I caught only one, though I landed plenty of salmon parr. Each day I was treated to new and exciting flies with which to break the jinx –

Blue Uprights, Coch-y-Bonddu's, Tup's Indispensables (what a lovely name to roll off a boy's lips), Wyckham's Fancies and Greenwell's Glories. On the last morning the Barle was in flood. 'We'll try the garden fly this morning', announced my new god. To a double hook an enormous worm was attached and Mr Tout slung it out. Our ambition was to catch a fish so large that it merited the description 'John Thomas'. Within a minute Mr Tout was into 'a real John Thomas'. I still remember the golden swirl before it came off. Later I caught one of three quarters of a pound, which Mr Tout assured me was one, though on the small side. It was taken home, with great pride, with pyjamas wrapped round it. My family's reaction, when I told them proudly that I had caught 'a real John Thomas', can be imagined.

I could find no more trout fishing until the discovery, a few years later, of a tiny stream at Maresfield in Sussex. Our peripatetic family had moved to Godstone and I started to visit what proved to be a little paradise, on the advice of a boy from school, round whose garden the nameless stream curled. Looking at the map now it looks as though Maresfield is about forty miles from Godstone; but on a Green Line Bus, No. 409, it might have been nearly as far as the Scottish border. Stopping every few hundred yards, it seemed, the double-decker ground its way to East Grinstead (the half way mark), and on across Ashdown Forest to Maresfield, with me getting off at the cricket ground and running down the road that went to Uckfield, and to the stream, carefully nursing my tin full of worms to make sure that they remained lively.

I am sure no one else ever fished, or even knew of, that tiny stream, because the trout took the worm as though delivered from heaven. They were strong fighters too, but not strong enough to contend with my thick gut and my springy fly rod. I never caught less than four, and they were all between eight and ten inches long, great fish indeed by my standards. Those days were so exciting that a five hour journey in a smelly bus was no drawback; nor could I sleep the night before, or even the night after.

It was beginning, at last, to dawn on me that there were more acceptable ways of fishing. I was catching roach, rudd and chub on fly, and the excitement of the seen take and the tightening of the line was growing. I was also sensible enough to realise that trout are such fools for a worm, that its use could endanger the whole resident stock. Let no one be under any doubt that a good wormer can clean out any trout pool, and a group of them, any river. Fishing is a sport that must be played (at least by grown-ups) according to rules and restrictions.

By the time war came I had fished in many places, in river and lake; almost entirely fly fishing, almost always for the infinitely desirable trout; but there were no Rutland and Grafham Waters then, and Blagdon was but a rumour, unapproachably distant. Even then I was developing a permanent ambition, (one not destined to be fully achieved) – a lovely licentious girl, possibly a nymphomaniac, living with me for life, in an old and comfortable house round which a clear, deep, fast-flowing trout stream gushed. We would no longer be poo-er, but very rich.

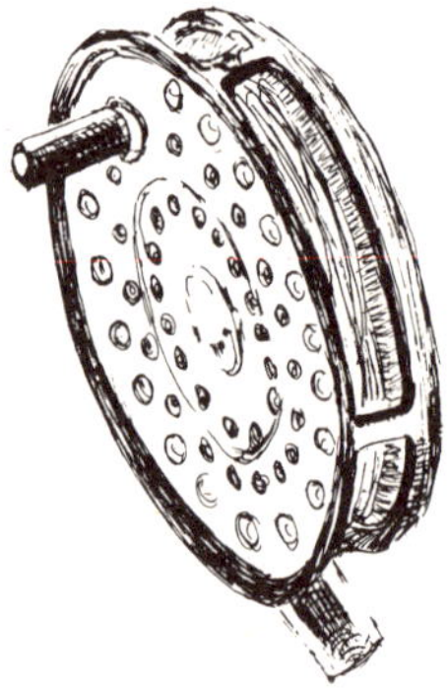

CHAPTER FOUR

Back to Hampshire

King and country gave me a lavish reward for my four and a half years servitude, by forgetting about me. I was happily ignored by the War Office and my leave stretched from May until 18th December when, having dug out my battledress, I set forth with a mixed crowd of fairly desolate soldiers for a posting to Germany. They had remembered that I had once qualified as a lawyer – and I was off to provide some legal services for which more than five years away from the law had left me unqualified. Much, however, had happened in my life since those first days back in Hampshire.

Apart from catching one or two fish of better size and quality than ever before, I had decided to continue my search for that impossibly attractive, substantially rich girl. The large country houses in the Winchester area were, I felt sure, filled with superb elder daughters who had little on their minds except to spend their lives with someone like me. Unfortunately such houses never opened their doors to twenty-seven-year-old temporary captains, because they never knew of their existence. After grappling with ladies met at the better bars, without a sign of all those marvellous emotions that the Hollywood dream factory had taught me to expect, I realised that in the years ahead there might be plenty of opportunities at that lower level, but few of the standard that the Fishing for the Forces was teaching me to expect.

Let me register, if I have never registered it before, my immense gratitude to Sir John Shelley-Rolls who commanded a long and lonely stretch of the Itchen at Itchen Abbas and who, in reply to my begging letter, replied – 'Delighted if you would come whenever possible'. Suddenly another superlative Nirvana was opened to me, not quite the same as the Test, but unique in character, and no less exciting. Here I learned of the marvels of an Itchen evening rise, when fish that had never been seen during the day, appeared from nowhere and rose heartily to nearly every cast. Here I learned too, under the careful eye of the keeper, the art of the nymph and the induced take. One evening I accidently strayed fifty yards too far downstream where I was attacked by someone who looked too much like the generals I had been avoiding since 1940. I told him it was certainly my fault, but he would have none of it. 'If that bloody Rolls would look after his river properly, nothing like this would happen'. No one was going to speak of my benefactor like that, so I gave him some most impertinent home truths, saying how sad it was that people who had spent their non-combatant wars in prime parts of Hampshire could not be a little more tolerant. I learned much too late that he was a World War I hero, deeply involved with the invention of the tank.

There were no troubles of any kind with my new best friend, Lord Louis Mountbatten. Well, not quite my new best friend, but his agent lavishly dealt me some quite remarkable days on the Broadlands fishing. I would book in for two nights at one of the Romsey hotels and arrive in time for dinner – muttering, as I signed in, about the Broadlands connection. There was always a chance, I felt sure, of a casual and romantic meeting with one of those lovely elder daughters – for here surely was a lovely elder daughter headquarters. But they were still kept under lock and key those days, protected, certainly, against romantic fortune hunters such as me.

The prime Broadlands beat, in my view, was Number Three, the beat nearest the tidal water, an early stopping place, I soon discovered, for incoming salmon and seatrout – a generous beat full of terrifying fishing problems. The thought of fishing for the salmon never crossed my mind. I did not even know how to set about it, yet these giant fish were sometimes visible in the clear water. I knew that they were quite easy to catch, for I had nearly caught one the only time I had salmon fished. (This had been at the beginning of the war in a tidal pool at Rhuddlan in North Wales. I had a tiny steel spinning rod, an American multiplying reel called a Nowaycanitfail and some silver spinners. I hooked this enormous salmon with my second cast and within a few minutes it was lying on its back ready for the slaughter. Unfortunately it was twelve feet below me. I could see no possibility of reaching it. Then the Japanese silk gut broke. I realise now that it must have been a kelt.) On the Mountbatten reaches of the Test, where it was Fly Only, such an unacceptable way of fishing was not conceivable, especially under the kind, steady, informative, but not entirely tolerant, eye of Mr. Geary, the keeper.

As those who have been lucky enough to enjoy it will know, a day on the Test is a day spent in search of a rising fish. In August there are not all that many of these, but there were enough surface movements to keep me happy as I waited for the evening rise. At lunch time I went back to the hotel for lunch (Romsey hotels did not seem to have trouble with rationing) and a pint of beer, with an eye cocked for stray elder daughters. On the third day I persuaded Melody to accompany me – a tall bright girl I had met recently in Winchester who was deeply involved in getting herself invalided out of the Wrens. She had never been on a fishing adventure before and was impressed with the river but disappointed by the apparent lack of activity. As dusk fell and we sat chewing locally made Cornish pasties and sipping Scotch she said, 'I'll tell you something – I've never got laid on the bank of a salmon pool'. This expression was new to me, a spillover from the Yanks, I guessed, but easy to understand. At that moment of decision, the river surface came alive – there was a monstrous hatch (or fall) of sedges. It was no contest. Melody lingered on, but our relationship was never again so potentially close.

On the last Broadlands day came the big adventure. There was a stain of colour in the water from the previous day's rain and my prospects, I thought, were not very good – but lo! at 8.30 sharp, the sedges once again started falling. It looked as though there was a rainstorm. At the top of the beat a fish began to rise with speed and enthusiasm, gurgles and rings and snatches. Unusually, it did not keep to the same spot, but wandered here and there in a feeding frenzy. It was some minutes before my sedge floated by on the right line – but as soon as it did, it was taken without hesitation. As I climbed out of the river, rod bent, I was treated to a display of jumping such as I had never previously seen. I saw it four or five times in the dusk, and knew I was into the fish of my lifetime. After a minute or two it decided on a change of tactics and started swimming downstream. Every hundred yards or so it stopped and turned and shook its head, then off it went again. I had crossed two fields and two stiles when I saw disaster thrusting towards me at a point where the river curled away and flowed the far side of a deep broad swampy bed of reeds. Once the fish was parted from me by this, I knew the game was lost. Summoning my waning energy and overcoming my quivering nerves I slowly and inexorably tightened on a very tired fish. It came slowly to the surface, hung in the current well out of reach, shook its head and drifted slowly away, the fly still in its mouth. I cannot remember whether or not I cried, but I was close to it. It was not a brown trout, of course, most probably a seven or eight pound seatrout, possibly a salmon. This estimate of its weight is a sober and informed one, made in the light of subsequent fishing adventures – a considerable reduction on the assessment I made at the time.

What I did catch at Broadlands was my personal record chub. I saw a shoal of these monsters cruising in a backwater one morning. I changed my Houghton Ruby for my friend the Caperer, soaked it so that it would sink, and offered this tempting mouthful to the chub. One took it and fought better than chub are supposed to. I put it back after weighing it on my moderately accurate scales, which it tipped at six pounds three ounces. I had not got the effrontery to record it in the Fishing Book.

The last major fishing in that summer of 1945 was in a lake at Northington. It was owned by Mr. Wallach who was glad to provide this worthy serviceman – then in the third month of his holiday – with all that his lovely lake had to offer. In a preliminary reconnaissance I had already noticed trout nymphing where a little stream came in, but Mr. Wallach was adamant. 'Dry Fly only' he said. To be fair to him I believe it was a parrot phrase, beause there was no possible prospect of catching any of the trout on dry fly. If one or two took nymphs, the remainder fed ferociously on the fry of roach.

The lake provided what must have been the best roach fishing in the United Kingdom. I soon laid down my fly rod and brought out my coarse fishing tackle and started catching these enormous unsophisticated fish. In one morning I caught three, each over two pounds, the kind of monsters which many dedicated and expert roach fishermen may catch only once in a lifetime. One day I killed four or five pound-size roach (I had been told to kill them all, but could not), and dropped them into a pub on the way home. If I had given away a load of venison it could not have been received with more pleasure. This was at a time when rationing was unrelenting and fresh fish – even roach – a delicacy. Big roach do not taste at all bad, once one has mastered the bones.

On the last day (also the last day of the trout season) I went again to the lake. I cast (for want of anything better) a large Coachman over an enormous cruising trout. Six times he ignored it. In a moment of extreme irritation I ran into the wood and started turning over tree stumps until I found a good fat worm. I attached this to my Coachman, spotted the monster again, 'cast' it over it and watched the white flash as the great mouth opened and closed. After a hectic splashing fight I netted it (I still carried a net in those days), and at that moment a delighted Mr. Wallach walked down the path towards me. 'This'll make a marvellous meal for you, Sir', I said respectfully. I broke the Coachman off the cast. 'You might like to keep the fly', I murmured unabashed. The worm had been swallowed. Two months or so later I read in *The Sporting and Dramatic* (much missed by people like me) of the catching of a brown trout of four pounds ten ounces at Northington, 'on a dry Coachman'. As I write this I am satisfied that my cheating days are over – yet none too confident that, if very deeply tempted, I could still remain pure.

Now that I appeared to have a future, I had been using some of the spare time in making urgent attempts to find myself a job after demobilisation. Through the good offices of the Law Society, I was put in touch with John Dawbarn, who practised at Wisbech in Cambridgeshire. I did not know where it was, but with the help of a map and a railway guide I reached it. After a friendly weekend I was promised employment as an assistant solicitor when demobilised. By that time I was able to encourage my employer by telling him that I would be bringing with me a delightful WRNS Admiral (or something nearly as grand) who would by then be my wife.

The Admiral had come quite recently into my life and seemed to fulfill all the requirements I had set for my future. Tall and willowy, blonde, voice slightly Knightsbridge, a small private income, a popular figure in her officers' clubs, coming out of the Navy any day and perfectly prepared to accept the engagement ring that had been returned to me by a very favourite lady in 1940, who had realised, just in time the mistake she had been on the verge of making. My family applauded warmly and the Admiral agreed to wait until I returned from Germany. I must admit that my blood cooled a little when she talked of morning suits and a wedding at St. Margaret's (or was it a church in Knightsbridge?), but before that dread moment there was one last spell in uniform.

CHAPTER FIVE

Post-War Germany

All good things come to an end, and with the trout season's finish came a letter from the War Office asking me to report to Room 897. Now I come to think about it, telling, not asking. A fine fellow, with his left breast covered with medal ribbons, passed the time of day before asking, 'Aren't you a qualified lawyer?' I explained that it went no further than passing my finals in early 1940 when they were letting through anybody who could fill a page or two of paper. When I had taken them the first time, in the summer of 1939, I had (they told me) got almost the lowest-ever recorded marks in some of the papers. (I was in America on a beach in Quogue, Long Island, lying with a girl named Helen, who was later to become Miss Star Spangled Banner, when the Western Union boy came running to me with a telegram. 'Failed. Come Home. Mum', it announced.) I did not pass on this anecdote to my man at the War Office who sent me a letter, a week or two later, telling me that I would be joining the army of occupation in Germany as a legal officer. Three weeks later still came the news that I had to make my way to Munster leaving the UK on 18th December – a sensational date in my life, for it had been on 18th December 1940 that I left Liverpool, shivering, for an undisclosed destination in the hold of the *City of London*, accompanied by a battalion of other dispirited members of the Royal Tank Regiment.

Going, this time, was very different. Germany was no longer a dangerous place. I travelled first class and even had my own army issue camp bed – though I do not think I took it with me. I certainly took my fly rod and some basic tackle. I remember little of the journey, or even of the Christmas that was soon to be celebrated – but the war was over and enormous weights had been lifted from all shoulders. After a few days at Munster – 'learning the form', they called it – I was given the choice of a posting between two places, one of which was Detmold. Noticing on the large scale·map at least three promising rivers or streams, I plumped for Detmold. It was the most sensationally significant and brilliant choice of my life.

I moved into a pleasant mess, surrounded by thoroughly laid back people and eased myself into the duties of a legal officer. They were not too arduous. I had to learn the existing Military Law – and apply it. The most public place where this happened was the Detmold Town Court – the equivalent of a magistrates' court, though we do not sentence respectable ladies to three months in jail for being out after curfew in our magistrates' courts. I had a Mercedes car and was involved in fascinating prosecutions (before real judges) involving rapes and murders. The time passed in an interesting fashion and on the not-too-distant horizon was the day when the army would finally let me loose.

Meantime my private life had not been prospering. The photograph by my bed of the Admiral, out of uniform, in twinset and pearls, began to look much less mesmerising – in dire contrast to the yearning German and Hungarian girls who were there for the taking. Worse was to come. The Admiral had made an unscheduled stop at Wisbech. She hated it (silly girl – I have now lived there for more than forty years and found each one of them marvellous), and had told me there could be no question of making our home there. This was a significant contribution (an explanation, perhaps, but hardly an excuse) to what followed.

One evening I and two others from my mess wandered aimlessly round to the officers' club. A German band was playing a kind of dance music, and duty-free drinks were being lavished into all the customers' glasses. On a raised section at the far end of the room were three very senior officers indeed – lieutenant-generals at the very least – chatting up the loveliest girl I had ever seen. She was dressed in the smart, eye-catching uniform of an American army captain. With no realisation of its significance I turned to my mates and said 'That's the lady I'm going to marry'. It was the signal for another round of drinks and a lot of laughter and remarks like, 'She's a mile out of your league'. Yet, miraculously after eight hair-raising weeks (including a lot of unhappiness with the Admiral), Marjorie and I walked up the aisle of the church at Detmold, the Movietone News cameras clicking (it was the first inter-allied wedding in post-war Germany), and all our friends assembled in optimistic surprise. 'Watch him', the best man had told her, (not without just a touch of envy, for he too thought she was marvellous) but I can only say, as I near the end of this chapter, that we have been magically happily married now, for more than forty four years.

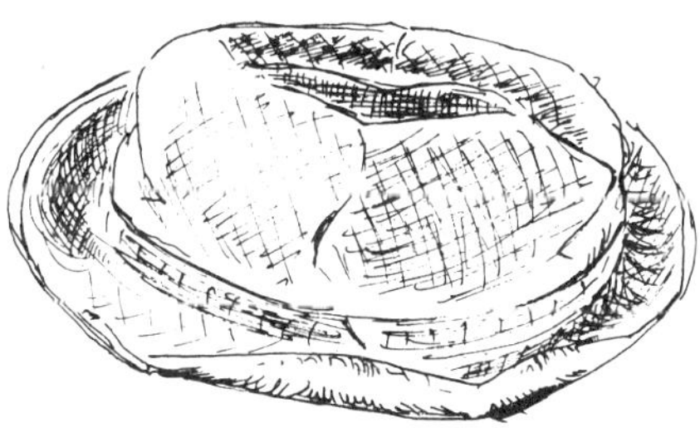

CHAPTER SIX

Marjorie

Marjorie came from the Nebraska prairies where her family are farmers. During the depths of the depression she had worked her way through university and medical school and got her MD. She gained a speciality in pathology, worked at Ann Arbor and then at Boston (where she lost a little of her mid-west accent), before joining the US Army. At the time we met, she was in charge of the medical services in an enormous Displaced Persons' Camp near Detmold – and I was sending a number of her patients to prison. There was good fishing in the River Platte, she told me, and she had a fish pole at home. It sounded funny the way she said it. What she liked much better than catching catfish, bass and carp were her horses. She had even taken one to the university with her (where she had been offered a job in a circus), and through all our life together we have had horses as well as fishing. I don't horse. She doesn't fish. I help clean the stables in winter; in summer – spring and autumn, too – we take fishing holidays.

The fishing near Detmold was very good. As soon as we could get away from work, off we would go. In one river there were trout and big grayling – we fished for them downstream, casting across diagonally with a pair of flies. We caught plenty. Then were was a clear, slow runing trout river beside which we sat and kissed and waited for the rises. A lovely photograph in our album shows us, the flowers and the river. That was one of the times I did not notice that the fish had started to rise. Germany, that April and May, was gleaming and brilliant. Beside her Mess in the forest ran a little stream.

I had been moved out of the HQ Mess in Detmold into the country to a nice little house a mile from hers. I used to run across to her at six in the mornings (before we moved in together), and catch her a trout or two for breakfast. She agreed that it was a lot better than catfish fishing. Yet another stream, I discovered, was full of lovely free-feeding trout up to about a pound. If I had not spent my time the summer before in Hampshire, on the cream of England's trout fishing, I would have been inclined to think that this was the best I had ever had. I would fish my way upstream, attacking the plentiful rising fish. When I had got far enough away from my car (and was telling myself that I really ought to have locked it), I would fish back with a wet fly downstream. Either way seemed equally effective. With hindsight I have come to believe that the conquerors were fishing in places that had been heavily stocked and preserved for the party leaders. There was not any other way in which it could have been so good.

We went for our first honeymoon to Mohne See, and on my oath I did not have fishing in mind: I merely wondered whether there was anything finny in that famous water. When the warden of the leave camp offered me a day's fishing, let it be permanently recorded, I turned it down. My wife and I, never missing a moment to catch up on those years without our love, had developed various stomach upsets that needed all the facilities the camp had to offer. We did stagger round to the end of the dam where the bombs had bounced, but in all other ways we behaved pretty sensibly, even when thirty of our new best friends from Detmold turned up on the Sunday afternoon.

My family had got over the shock of the broken engagement and was entranced at the thought of the American doctor who was entering our lives. My mother was rehashing every medical symptom that she had suffered in the last five years, looking ahead to endless discussions over glasses of sherry.

The rest of the family were mildly reserved; what will the man do next they wondered? Marjorie's family had sent us a famous and marvellous welcoming telegram on the wedding day, but the letter from my mother-in-law (who had expected her daughter, naturally enough, to be practising in Nebraska) summed it all up. 'When I read your news, I could have cried'. She had previously met only one Englishman, and he had disappeared with the Forces' Benevolent Fund that she had had under her charge.

After Marjorie had met – and dazzled – the family, we set off on our real honeymoon in Scotland. It was the first of dozens of very happy journeys across the border. We went to the Trossachs Hotel after reading a note about it in a Sunday paper (comfort, plentiful food, fishing and walking) and, still being in the forces, travelled first class, for just about the last time in our lives.

First class carriages have not changed all that much over the years, though then they were cleaner than they are now. Just four very well-sprung seats on each side, with moveable arm rests and individual lights – even a heat regulator if all occupants could agree on its use. On top, of course, the net luggage racks. What must have been quaint were the clothes we wore, which looked as if they had come from a well-found jumble sale. Clothing was rationed; new clothes were not available for love or money. I had what was left of what I wore as an impecunious articled clerk. Strange things like a dinner jacket and cricket trousers had survived; there were a few thick woollen and poplin shirts; my suits had vanished. I had, however, received my demob suit, a brown two-piece job, made of some very inferior tweed, a shirt or two and even a tie. Somehow or other I could put enough together to be allowed into a hotel. My wife could either wear her smart, well-fitting army uniform, or khaki slacks, or such bounties as my family had loaned her.

In our carriage it would have been difficult to squeeze a

penny between us. The only other passengers were two missionaries returning from Africa, judging by their luggage labels. They were not on such coy terms as we were. At five in the morning, as we approached Berwick, Mrs. Missionary stretched upwards to get her toothbrush (or shaving things) from the luggage rack, standing on the seat to do so. As she struggled with the case, her knickers, red ones, betrayed her and slipped own to her ankles. My wife, full of good intentions, gave the lady a nudge, as she didn't appear to realise what had befallen her. Mrs. Missionary, thinking herself to be in danger of some sort of base assault, retaliated with a backhander that would have taken the head off a bullock. But you don't catch a Nebraskan cowgirl that easily, and the swipe hit only the air. As we sat back and watched, the knickers, wrenched off the feet, were put into the open suitcase. I could feel the shaking beside me. Behind our newspapers we suppressed our laughter till it hurt and just as one was calming down the other started again. When at last the missionaries got out (looking affronted for some reason) we rolled about on the seat with giggles we no longer had to suppress until the train reached Calendar. From there we caught a bus to the Trossachs.

It was unthinking of me to have brought my fishing rod, except that I had the feeling that in Scotland fish were everywhere. I soon found out that the only fish in the loch opposite the hotel were perch. Then we borrowed bicycles and biked to Loch Catrine. Marjorie was not good on a bicycle and the journey was perilous; she ran into a sheep that, she said, looked like her sister Betts. We hired a boat and somehow persuaded the steamship *Sir Walter Scott* to tow us into the loch. I fished as she rowed back. The rowing could not have done her much good because the next day when we were half way up a small mountain, she was stricken by terrible pains – and had a miscarriage. Not many wives can safely diagnose their own miscarriage. I kept asking, after two minutes, 'Are you OK? Are you sure we oughtn't to get you to a hospital?' and she kept saying she was fine. We went to bed after lunch that day and she woke up saying she was a new woman. 'I was thinking we could bike to Calendar', I said, 'but now we could get a taxi – it would be fun to see if we could catch a seatrout in the River Teith'. Suddenly I saw, carefully concealed as it was, a little sign of weariness in the face of my beloved – the sign of someone who wonders if she may be about to spend a lifetime trotting along behind a fishing fool. The journey was cancelled.

We had three more marvellous days before we returned to Micheldever and she went on to Germany. She was away for a desolate three weeks while I moved myself to Wisbech, having explained to my employer that there had been a change of matrimonial plans. We had a week together (no fishing) before she returned to America to get out of the forces and to collect, as she put it, her clothes. During the forty-two days she was away (explaining me to her family, escaping from the forces – 'one of the nation's finest' President Truman called her in a note that still hangs in our downstairs lavatory – and fixing up her return journey) I nearly went mad. Communications were impossible at the time and I had convinced myself that she would never come back, when the cable came from the *Queen Mary*. The day she returned with an enormous trunk full of surprises, was one of the most supremely happy of my life. I had found a flat in which we could start our life together – and our contentment knew no bounds.

I was torn, that winter, between catching up on a legal career that had never even begun, trying to understand what a lawyer's job really was, attempting to break into the close circle of lawyers in Wisbech where the war had hardly affected legal life – and spending as much time as I could with her. Temptation! The flat was only 200 yards away from the office – half a minute at a quick trot. I tended to arrive at work a little later in the morning than I should and escape too soon in the evenings. I was holding myself out as a court lawyer on the strength of my experiences in Detmold. The court laywer, or advocate par excellence, in the area was Mr. Pettefar, who knew far too much for me in those very early days and who almost invariably left me feeling foolish and inept. One Saturday (we worked on Saturdays) a wiry Fenman called to see me, brandishing a poaching summons returnable at Methwold on the following Monday. I took a proof from him and told him that, with travelling, it would cost him £10. 'Is that all?' he asked looking pleased. Somehow or other I achieved an acquittal. My client came up to me, beaming. 'I shall always know where to come in future, Mr. Pettefar', he said – which explained his pleasure at my fee. Pettefar was said to be very costly.

Our stimulating life continued and the time drew close when we were going to have to make up our minds whether to stay in Wisbech or move on. Marjorie had been busily qualifying (there being no total reciprocity between American and English medical systems) and there would clearly be a lot of demand for her services. 'All I need', I murmured, 'is some proper fishing'. A life of roach and bream from the Fenland rivers (others would call them canals) was not going to sustain me.

We bought an ordnance map and traced in it the rivers in Norfolk that looked as if they had trout potential – rivers like the Wensum, the Wissey and the Stiffkey. Then we wrote to the big houses near their banks. The infant Wensum seemed promising on inspection. It belonged to the Marquess of Townshend. I looked up how to do it and wrote a begging letter to My Lord Marquess. I refrained from adding Major to my signature. The rank seemed minute by comparison. Anyway, of course, I did not use it. The reply was charming. 'Certainly', he wrote, 'there are a few trout – look in and have tea'. It was a delightful answer, but he was out when we called. My wife had a close look at an Inigo Jones hall of great magnificence – but the trout were indeed too few and far between.

Then one Sunday, on fishing patrol, we saw a little river which passed under the road to Docking and flowed into a lake. In the clear water, in the top pool, I saw a number of trout, some over a pound. The mansion in the park was decayed and empty. When the village vicar (God bless him) answered my letter, he told me where to go and who to see. I drove in, full of nerve, a week later, just as she got back from church. The vicar's tip was spot on. I told her my tale quickly. I told her truthfully, that if I did not have good fortune soon, we would leave for Dartmoor or the Lake District. 'I think we'll keep you here, Mr. Barr', she answered, 'next summer you may come four times'. And that is how I was allowed onto my beloved Babingley. Very sadly, she died at the end of the summer – but her successor allowed those who had fished that year to organise themselves into a sort of syndicate. Marjorie would be the first to agree that during the years I have been fishing there, there has been more than one occasion when escape to the Babingley has been a veritable life saver.

Our lives were filled with continuous pleasures. Quarrels? We never had one. A silence once or twice, but never a raised voice. It is only possible to say this publicly because the truth is apparent. Even so there were many days, weeks and months when all kinds of pressures gripped us both, and even talk of fishing (for example) had to be pushed into the background.

Three years in the ranks proved to have been a fine investment. I was equipped to get along easily with the widest range of people. There is no Fenland aristocracy, but there are plenty of very bright and clever people and there are also many warm friendly ones who are glad to cast their problems at you, saying, 'I must leave it to you, Mr. Barr: I'm no scholar'. Ability to meet peoples' minds (rather than legal genius) has been a surefire factor in the building up of a legal practice. In those days lawyers were constantly on the lookout for any form of touting or self-advertisement. I had to do my building by impressing the public that I was alert, easily approachable and very swift – without my motives being suspect. The practice certainly needed building, with a total pay roll, including me, of seven (and something must have finally happened for we now have two offices and forty-two people working in them. We are also allowed, as can be seen, to advertise). After a few years we had moved from the flat to Mill House (corn mill: no stream), and mortgage commitments had become an anxious pain in the back of our necks.

Meanwhile Marjorie, duly qualified, had started her own practice. The scullery at Mill House had been converted into a surgery, the adjoining outhouse into a waiting room. Patients poured in. Lady doctors were still rare. Brand new American doctors, even rarer. Wickedly I let it be hinted (falsely) that she had access to all kinds of American drugs. It made no difference at all: the patients were already in love with her. Within eight weeks 750 National Health patients had signed onto her list. When she refused to take more she became an even more desirable property. The income from the practice was £750 a year, more or less. It was enough to bring in eighteen-year-old Bonnie as housekeeper and watcher of the two boys. The balance went on Marjorie's car. It was not riches, but was certainly fulfilling. Bonnie, now a well-loved family friend, still works for us two mornings a week. Our lives would have been disastrously different without her.

As my own work load grew, pressures accumulated. Being a lawyer may not be so exacting if you know all the answers. I knew few of them. During my first fifteen years I should have walked round with an L on my back. Every problem needed time and thought – but people do not like prevarication. Inspired guesses are rarely good ones. Work bit into Saturdays and Sundays and much of our time together. John Dawbarn was tragically killed in 1951. I was left alone in the practice – with every possibility that there would be no practice in a year's time. I took on the job of Coroner, which John had graced for many years, not because I liked the job, but because £300 a year was pretty desirable at the time. Being Coroner is no sinecure. One must be available at all times, to cope with sudden and unexplained deaths. I never enjoyed the misery and earned a name for holding the quickest inquests on record. The best part was my relationship with the police. All young constables were liable to be pulled in as Coroner's Officer, taking statements, arranging post mortems, reporting to me. I never came across one who did not measure up to his difficult task. The years finally brought relief in the shape of able partners. A lawyer on his own is only half a man. He is more than twice that with good men and women around him.

Marjorie, meantime, after twenty years of shedding heart's blood on her patients' behalf (those were the days when you went to the homes to deliver babies) decided, one autumn morning, to give it all up, join the hospital service and start screening for cancer. She had been involved, in the very earliest days, in cytology, at Ann Arbor. In her final year of full time work she organised four open Well Women Clinics and was dealing with endless thousands of cervical smears. There are many who owe her much.

We used to read wingeing articles and listen to shrill radio talks on the impossibility of combining career and family. For the record, she managed it all with grace and kept all the Barrs contented and filled with admiration – including, of course, our two sons.

My runaway pen has so far made no mention of Richard, born just over a year after we were married, and William, born two years later – the two most perfect apples of Marjorie's eye. Every word written so far – and most of those to come – is affected by the joys and burdens and stimulations and challenges of their upbringing. They never missed anything through their mother's involvements. On the contrary, she is the living proof that a busy person is the person who has a little extra time for everything.

CHAPTER SEVEN

Salmon. The Start

I asked Marjorie today if I could possibly have contracted Altzheimer's Disease, but she said, 'No, no worry about that'. I had been taken aback because, less than forty years after the event, I could not remember the exact details of our first fishing journey to the Wye.

In those very earliest days, with our two practices a long way from being profitable, we were not all that far from the breadline. We were earning about £10 a week between us.

Then a pair of friends asked us to go with them and spend a long weekend in Herefordshire. The hotel, Brookhampton Court, had available 'a famous salmon beat'. It also had a stable of horses. Our friends who were rich, handed us an envelope the night before we set off. In it were four £5 notes and the message 'Use in the bar'. If you live in the Fens, surprises of this sort are not rare and the tact of our friends made it easy for us. With a formidable ex-nurse looking after the boys, we went away with light hearts, the most ambitious treat we had had since our honeymoon – and another first for the doctor from Nebraska. We shared our friends' Rover (they called them four-seaters in those days) and made our way over narrow roads (not a motorway in sight) to Herefordshire, poring over maps and occasionally losing our way.

Forgetting the fishing for a moment, it could not have been a more enjoyable holiday, with big, well-cooked meals and ancestral hall elegance. We were in tune with our friends and held our own in the bar. It would have been difficult to spend all the £20 on rounds of drinks in those lower priced days, so it made a nice dent in the hotel bill as well. Beer was a shilling (5p) a pint – a large scotch half a crown (12½p).

The Wye looked, at first sight, like a quicker moving, more curvaceous imitation of the higher reaches of the Thames. Balsam was in flower along its banks; cows grazed, people swam. I knew so little about salmon fishing, water heights, temperatures and taking times, that I did not realise the hopelessness of it all. The river was running through clusters of waving weeds, the only obvious water movement being where it ran freely between the weed-channels. There was indeed the occasional very heavy *splosh* from a potted salmon; so little did I know that I was sure that anything that moved must be catchable. The famous salmon beat would have looked very different in February, March and April.

Marjorie had been out on one of the hotel horses, but was back in time to demonstrate, once again, her rowing skills as we crossed the river to fish the top of the beat from the right bank. I had been lent a twelve-foot fly rod, reel and line, and I had discovered somewhere or other a little creche of large, old fashioned, single-hooked salmon flies, tied with infinite skill and precision, with names like Jock Scott, Durham Ranger and Mar Lodge. Stealthily, in my new thigh waders, I crept into the water, the most naive and underskilled salmon fisherman ever to enter the Wye. At my third cast there was a hefty pull and a splash and my rod bent double as I tried to heave out the monster. I could feel the throbbing of the fish through the bank of weeds into which it had plunged. At that moment Marjorie shouted 'Hang on!', and brandishing a borrowed gaff she leapt into the river, way over her riding pants, in the direction of the action. Suddenly, alas, the pressure subsided and over the weed bed slithered a rather exhausted three pound chub. For some reason, I have ever since tended to regard the Wye as a very good chub river.

I cannot resist one other memory of the Wye. One of our local doctors was holidaying near Hay. He had never fished in his life, but a close friend asked him to try his hand on a good beat.

He proved to be a good pupil and on his fifth sling, he caught one. I never heard an independent account of the excitements involved, but he told the story like this. 'There I was with the fishing rod in my hand. They tied on something called a Yellow Belly. I hoicked it across the river. Next thing I knew it had been swallowed, so I wound it in.' 'But what was it?', I asked, meaning what weight. 'Oh, it was a… er…salmon, I think.' He never fished again and hardly deserved to.

Even before my first encounter with the Wye, I had met that lovely man Walter Whiting, at the time just about the most distinguished chartered accountant in East Anglia. He, too, fished the Babingley and it was he who pointed me seriously in the direction of salmon. He had a rod on the Yorkshire Esk where they were, at that time, killing fish in great numbers – as I know now, far too great; nothing was barred except cyanide, explosives and nets. Prawn, shrimp, worm and spinner were all in high fashion. No one could have been more generous than Walter – in every way – in helping and inspiring a fairly young and totally inexperienced novice.

Walter used to get telephone calls from David Cook the river keeper on the Esk, employed by the Esk Fishery Association. David was an energetic young man, newly out of the military police, full of hopes and ambitions for the river, and admired by one and all; always a lively and smart figure on his motor bike. However many things he had to do, he always had time to help anyone in need. Whenever Walter heard from him, it was to be told that there was a flood in the river and that the fish were running. The Esk was going through a wet-weather phase and the floods were not the rarities they afterwards became. After one such telephone call he asked me to come with him – and I was taken by car up the A.1 (the old A.1, with narrows and bends and lorry drivers' pull-ins), through York, and on over the North Yorkshire Moors, via Malton and Pickering, to Grosmont, where we stayed at the Station Hotel. It was 170 miles and the journey took a day.

Like the raising of a theatre curtain, the Esk was gently revealed to me – quite wide, quite swift in places, a brown river running through thickly-treed shale valleys and woodland. I was shown some of its famous pools – Bridge, Balcony, Dead Man, Gilson's – and I saw for the first time the movements of hosts of huge running fish. As I looked down from the top of a bank on the very first morning, something that seemed as big as a porpoise swam gently by, and, as its back curved, I could swear I heard it sigh. This, I thought, must be just about the most exciting place in the world.

The Association rule was that a member could bring with him a very limited number of guests in a season, but could not fish at the same time. Both the days I was there, Walter refused to fish. Later on I was to realise that he received as much pleasure from seeing his guest catch a fish as if he had been fishing himself. That is known as unselfishness.

I was lent a spinning rod and a fixed spool reel and spent the first day learning to cast. It was not all that difficult – at least to do it badly – and by the evening I had lost eight Devon Minnows and caught nothing. 'Spin slowly' they kept telling me and I did – right onto the rock and shale on a bottom that grabbed a spinner like a magnet.

Just before lunch on the second morning, spinning technique improving each minute, there was a huge swirl and pull and I found that I had hooked a salmon and a big one. It created waves as it bolted round the pool; then, still hooked, but totally in control of affairs, it set off upstream. I followed it as best I could, trying to come to terms with the slipping clutch, handing the rod to helpers as I passed bankside trees. I had a clear view of a broad brown back when the hook came out. 'Twenty pounds if it weighed one', a sad Yorkshire voice murmured. In the distance I saw Walter walking swiftly away, head down, a broken man. He appeared an hour later, smiling once more. 'I went to the Arncliffe Arms', he whispered, 'and had five double gins.'

CHAPTER EIGHT

Into Dartmoor

The boys were in the range of seven and five when we went on our first holiday to Holne Chase, circled by the Dart, in heaven knows how many exciting acres of secluded, private woodland, and where, according to the advertisements, there was fly fishing for salmon – and horse riding. Before Marjorie had her own horses, finding animals that were reasonably interesting for her to ride, or, on lesser creatures, idyllic bridle paths and journeys, was as important as finding fishing. We found horses on Dartmoor and some interesting riding, which complemented the fantastic excitements of the Dart fishing. Quite a lot of years later a friend offered her a famous Arab stallion, Nizzolan, for a fifty-mile endurance ride on Dartmoor, in which she (or Nizzolan) won top marks. Perhaps it was her early explorations of the tors, bogs and hut circles that put her right. The horse, of course, got the credit.

The hotel at that time was brilliantly run by Eileen Dagger, a lady who had rescued the very beautiful house from dissolution, and created exactly our kind of hotel out of nothing very much. It may not then have had rooms with bathrooms, but it was warm, its public rooms were garlanded with flowers, it was reasonably priced, its food was substantial, its guests were honoured – and there was indeed some salmon fishing.

The real fishing, the cream, was to be found between Holne Bridge and New Bridge, three miles or so of superlative small salmon river in the loveliest of settings. This part was all, at that time, in the hands of a very high-powered syndicate. The generals had to move aside for the field marshals; and there were some distinguished stockbrokers and one fine local from Torquay as well. It was also, in those distant days, prime spring fishing. The salmon fishing available to us was not quite so good. Mrs. Dagger had retreated from the heat of the hotel's kitchen to a lovely Dart-side bungalow, surrounded that first time by rhododendrons of every conceivable colour, in dazzling clusters. Having advertised the available fishing she let us fish the beat that went with the bungalow, called, poetically, Queen of the Dart.

It was in Queen of the Dart that I spent the final peaking energies of my swiftly receding youth. I have fished hard and frantically since, but never on the scale of that first holiday in Dartmoor. I would leave our bed at five, drive swiftly towards Ashburton and down the gravelled road to the fishing. There were about three pools, the names of all of which I have forgotten – except the lowest one, the Black Pool I think it may have been called. Back for breakfast, then down again by ten, fishing through till one or two – and then back to a sandwich lunch with the family. We spent the afternoon together, walking over the moors, trying out the excitements of Torquay and Paignton Zoo, back to tea at the hotel, a bath, a drink, dinner, then off to the evening fishing. Marjorie would never let me go alone to that, so dark and sinister did the Black Pool look – and those were the times when we started to catch peel and seatrout.

I was learning hard, and the very first thing I learned was that it was a piscatorial and social blunder to start fishing the Black Pool until the general (another one) had arrived. I supposed that the war had left us all a bit bemused by generals (and surviving generals may have been around in unusually large numbers). We sat there in the dark, smoking our cigarette surreptitiously (we shared them, alternate puffs), until, from the wood across the river, we could hear the put-put-put of a small motor cycle. There was a rustling in the undergrowth (like a tiger starting its patrol) and a voice from the blackness shouted, 'Start to fish'. As it spoke there was an instantaneous swish – as his first cast reached the water before anyone else's.

Night fishing for seatrout is an elegant affair. After selecting the right fly, or flies (and whoever can say which they are – small and slightly bushy is my own recipe), one casts into the blackness. During the day, if wise, the fisherman will have tested the parameters of his cast, finding the place where the back cast will entangle with nothing that will interrupt the forward. The line creeps downstream in the current and nothing happens. Thirty yards away there's a splash and a gleam on the water as a seatrout moves. (A great seatrout expert, Arthur Oglesby, has described it better than I ever can.) Suddenly a small hand from nowhere pulls the unseen fly and there are explosions followed by minutes of the most intense excitement. The seatrout you think you are stopping running out of the pool leaps twenty yards upstream. Your line is in a huge submerged hoop. You put on upstream pressure – to find that the fish, all five pounds of it perhaps, has shot downstream, pulled out the fly and is making an uninterrupted way to safer and deeper lies.

Some beats fish better from one bank than the other. On Queen of the Dart we were in the favoured place, standing just above the tail of the pool, where the river disappeared into the wood, heading for Buckfast Abbey. We caught a few of the smaller peel, bid courteous goodnights to the assembled military on the far bank, and crept back to the bungalow and our car. All these drinking years later it now seems a little remarkable that we returned contentedly to bed in an unlicensed hotel and without a bottle in the bedroom.

Night fishing breeds stories of terror or disaster. One pitch dark night, a fishing friend, after Deveron seatrout in fairly high water, hooked something monstrous which he played for thirty five minutes, losing ground all the time – until he finally beached a large, white, plastic bag. Another hair-raising adventure happened to me on the River Conwy near Betws y Coed. The Conwy attracts – or certainly used to – some enormous seatrout, of the same size and class as the revered Dovey. When the fish are in, it is sometimes necessary to have a thin rod, with flies whistling into the river from both banks. I had taken up a position near some good lies with Marjorie and two holiday friends – with three rods between us. Waiting for the last daylight to go, I had leant my rod against a tree, the flies dangling in the night air. Suddenly the rod crashed to the ground and the line started to run off the reel. A passing bullock had not been able to resist my Invicta and was taking off with the fly firmly in his lip. It was then that my two friends and my cowgirl wife showed their metal. Typically, my contribution was limited to holding the rod – I am frightened of bullocks. One of the friends was a well-built farmer, the other a stout-hearted vicar. Making all kinds of soothing noises they halted the bullock, and while Marjorie and the farmer held the animal's hindquarters, the vicar, with an angel's skill, put his arms around its neck and, with a dramatic snatch, whipped the fly out of its mouth. The mildly perplexed but good natured beast wandered off, and I neither had my rod broken nor lost my fly. Not surprisingly I heard, some years later, that the vicar had become a bishop – clearly the kind of man the church is in need of. Ambitious clergymen should take note.

One afternoon when we were swapping cigarette puffs in the long hotel sitting room, wondering if there would be Devonshire cream with the tea and promising the boys at least half an hour's reading of *The Hound of the Baskervilles*, a tall lively man on a nearby sofa asked 'Any fish?' 'No', I answered, 'but not for want of trying.' One of the syndicate had returned that day with four. I was sick with frustration. Each one of them may have passed me. 'There'll be no one on the middle fishing the day after tomorrow', he said, 'I've got to go to

Torquay – so why don't you fish my rod for the day?' When the earth had stopped spinning I gasped, 'How could I ever thank you enough?' He answered smiling, 'You could tell me why you share cigarettes – health or economy?'

I still had not caught a salmon on a fly, though I had fished enough to realise that fly-caught salmon are the most worthily attained victims. The previous summer I had answered an advertisement in *The Field*, from an Aberdeen estate agent, offering salmon fishing in Scotland in July (a month that was historically deemed a disaster on the greatest Scottish rivers). Daring to the point of idiocy, I proceeded to hire, for a week, Inchmarlo – a beat of the very highest category just upstream of Banchory – for £10. It turned into one of the great holidays. Low water and burning sunshine got the whole family onto the banks of the Dee, the boys paddling, their mother getting a snatch of the kind of heat she had once enjoyed at home every day, every summer. I fished in gym shoes and shorts, wading all over the river under the benign eye of my first gillie, Mr. Wilkie. A week with him was a week of education. I was beginning, by the sixth day, to understand about a fly's water speed and the angles at which it should be cast, about the ways of discerning the hopes and avoiding the pitfalls. I caught three small grilse that low-priced week (which even then seemed a ridiculous bargain), and lost another five. It was dream fishing and it broke my heart when the owner did not repeat the offer next year – but who can blame him? Inchmarlo for £10! It might be £1,000 now at the best moments and only then if one was very lucky.

When, therefore, I stumbled down the paths from the hotel to the Dart's Middle Chase beat (if you run, as I did, you are bound to stumble) I had caught some grilse – but as far as a real salmon on fly was concerned, I was still a virgin.

There is little that is rarer or more attractive than to find yourself with a mile or two of unoccupied salmon fishing, every inch of it at your disposal. Even if you do not know the lies and taking places – or even the pools – it is still going to produce many breathless moments. Furthermore the family was going to walk down to these hallowed places and we were going to have a picnic lunch on the river bank. There had been rain; the Dart was slightly coloured, but dropping; I knew enough to be certain that conditions could hardly be bettered. What I was not at all sure about was what fly and what size to use. In the cold, late spring water, fish, if any, were not showing. It was a matter of carefully fishing every yard (where and when possible – my casting technique was strictly right shoulder and the background branches did not encourage this), and hoping something might go right. One of the residents had told me to imagine that my fly was a daddy-long-legs and to urge it across the pool with the help of the current. They all tend to move the fly in the West Country, but not, curiously, in the North. Nowadays I try various ways. I tried the propelled way, that day.

We had a picnic-lunch in front of a lovely looking pool where the current flowed round the line of rocks on the opposite bank – the stream being parted from me by several yards of back-eddy – by no means an easy place to fish. As we chewed our way through the ham sandwiches and kept the boys, bluffed by the threat of thrashings, under control, a big brown body curved through the top of the running water on the far side of the river. With trembling hand I tied on a Silver Doctor (I no longer have one in my box) cast across, did a mend so feeble that it was not recognisable as such and ... *zung* ... the line pulled off the reel as a salmon moved downstream, accommodatingly pulling my fly into its scissors. Verging on a heart attack, hands shaking so hard that the taut rod tip trembled, I eventually got this suicidal fish to my bank. I then produced the gaff that Marjorie had once wielded with such spirit on the Wye and hooked out the fish. It weighed ten pounds and seemed the most beautiful creature I had ever seen. My host would only take half of it and I drove home the next morning with the booty in the boot, a sophisticated successful catcher at last, that first hurdle fairly effortlessly leaped. Incidentally, I have never gaffed another fish and would be pleased to see gaffs made unlawful. If it means the loss of an occasional forty-five pounder, too bad.

During the next eight years we came to Dartmoor every April. This was a time when the year's holiday ration was two or, exceptionally, three weeks. The Dart needs water like a camel. The low Dart is a dead loss, more or less unfishable, hope of a salmon non-existent. The precious seven days would creep by – picnics and point-to-points were no real compensation – and at the end there were fifty more weeks without salmon fishing. It poured all of one of our last nights. When we left, at crack of dawn, I could see that the river was rising. I nearly wept.

Another time we spent a complete holiday – two whole weeks – at Holne Chase and got no fishing at all. On the other hand there were some great successes – two fish one Easter Monday morning (and another lost); a nineteen-pounder, tailed with the help of the whole family at Upper Corner Pool in a snowstorm; a nine pounder which jerked the tailer out of my hand as I was going to land it, and which cruised round the pool with the cork handle bobbing behind it till Marjorie seized it at the lip of the pool, the boys clasping her ankles – great times; the days of the Hairy Mary (the fly that the regulars scored with). I had a collection of Hairy Marys in all shapes, and made wise remarks like, 'There's only the need for this one fly, with size variations'. I doubt if I have any in my box nowadays. All the good fisherman needs are long-tailed stoats' tails, tied on outpoint treble hooks, with size and colour variations; that is my current fad. Who can tell – Hairy Marys may come back into fashion.

Our long romance with Holne Chase ended on a surprising note. Our party that year had grown, and we were also taking some care of a sister whose husband had just died. As she sat down to pour a cup of tea for herself and chew some of the hotel's famous sandwiches, a tiny grey lady crossed the room, whipped the cigarette from my sister's hand and threw it on the fire. People were smoking in those days without ignominy. We stared in amazement and I saw the young starting to laugh. 'What on earth do you think you are doing?', my sister asked, in her dowager, bazaar-opening voice. 'We never allow smoking at the Palace', was the unexpected reply. It turned out that she was not actually a member of the royal family, but had just retired from royal service. Within the next twenty-four hours the action quickened. She took to primping the cushions on our chairs as soon as we rose, rebuking the boys for the dirt on their shoes, and making remarks like, 'We'd never allow people in to dine with unkempt hair like yours'.

The following morning a note appeared pinned to the dining room door. It was called, 'An Ode to Miss Moore'. It was full of classical (but totally meaningless) references, and read a bit like the poem that begins, 'Lars Porsena of Clusium'. We were really quite a respectable group, but when she muttered, as she passed us at dinner, comments such as, 'Your manners are disgusting', and, 'I wonder you don't lick your knives', war was close to declaration. Meantime someone had started the brilliant operation on a vase of carnations – artificial ones. With great skill she transferred white petals to the pink ones and vice versa. We saw the management debating the alterations (suggesting that some chemical change was taking place) and we hinted that the guilty party might be Miss Moore taking it out on the plastic flowers because they never had them at the Palace. After that one of the boys loaded a can on a lavatory door which was designed to pour water on the inmate as he or she came out (it was genuinely aimed at a new best friend of fourteen, called Charlotte); it fell upon Miss Moore and the fat was in the fire. We left a day early with the words, 'You won't be welcome here again', ringing in our ears. Miss Moore had won and we heard later that the Dart valley was to ring with wild rumours of those days – rumours that included black magic, criminal assault and a witch-like terrorisation by the Barr family.

That was the end of the Dart fishing, but we have returned to Holne Chase – which is still able to offer its residents the lower slice of the Dart fishing (including the famous Chase Pool). The new owners welcomed us with apprehension (by this time we had grandchildren with us), but they found we were nothing like as bad as the stories – legends – had indicated.

If the Dart is not fishing well, there is, particularly in summer, the Duchy water to move to. It stretches nearly as far as Three Bridges, is triflingly cheap, is full of small brown trout and at times produces salmon and seatrout. There are people who live beside the moor who know all its secrets and conjure brown trout of ten ounces or more out of the tiny brooks – there are also one or two salmon pools that regularly hold fish. I recommend in particular Queenie, just above Dartmeet. One afternoon, as I fished it, Marjorie lay on the bank and gasped as she saw a salmon, with infinite delicacy, take my fly – then spit it out. The enthusiast at the reel end of the rod did not know anything had happened until he heard her gasp. This probably happens more often than we think.

CHAPTER NINE

Into Scotland

We moved, in the late 1950's, from our Dart stronghold, to holidays on the Deveron, the next river with which we were to develop a bond.

A couple of years previously I had introduced Jack Bridger to fishing, and he was drugged by it; ready to abandon wife, children and job to grasp a few previous days.

A knowing fruit and potato merchant from Scotland (for whom I was acting) had spoken to me out of the side of his mouth, with lots of winks and the occasional stroke of his nose with the first finger of his right hand, of marvellous spring fishing on the Deveron, on the Huntly burgh waters, costing next to nothing. It had been a long winter, and one March evening (having persuaded our wives that a break would do us all the good in the world) they drove Jack and me to catch the night train from Grantham. Even that fifty mile drive was a bit of an epic, so primitive were the roads at that time; there was no question at all of our trying to take on the two-day car journey to Aberdeen.

We were still novice salmon fishermen. I had a ten-foot split cane rod – too short and too heavy – and on my reel was a Kingfisher line that had to be dried at night and covered with mucilin, when dry, to make it float. I had not even graduated into chest waders (without which no salmon fisherman is properly equipped); I was still dodging about the edges in thigh waders, one eye on the line, the other apprehensively watching the water about to go over the top. Naturally Scotland in March demanded all kinds of warm clothes –

scarves, sweaters, thick woollen socks, stocking hats to be worn commando fashion. We both travelled with enough gear to keep us going in an Alaskan winter.

The railways in those days were the principal way of reaching all the Scottish fishing. No land rovers or range rovers were yet available. The old A.1 had one piece of dual carriageway on the north side of Newcastle, if you were lucky enough to break through that far, but it was far easier to take the train (I sometimes think it still is). Aberdeen station was the place where the heart started to beat faster. The platform in the mornings was speckled with tall, gaunt, very upright tweedy men. Someone else was carrying their luggage, for they strolled unencumbered, except by the most wandlike of fly rods, three slender split cane joints in Hardy Brothers' cases (even in those days there were reprobates who put lesser rods in those aristocratic cases). The main flow of fishermen was making for the Dee, or perhaps the Don (there were fine runs of salmon in those days) – but having come so far it was surely to waters below Banchory, or very much downstream of Ballater (and certainly Inchmarlo), to which those expensive tweeds were proceeding.

Jack and I would not (to the detached observer) have created such an enviable impression. We were carrying a lot of heavy gear, our clothes were not all that elegant, but at least we had no spinning rods in our hands. We were not being met at Aberdeen by large cars and retainers – and we were heading for the station restaurant where we were to have the first of several marvellous breakfasts (the grilled haddock was still twitching) – passing the time till we caught the slow train to Huntly.

There we were met, by my client's local representative who had got it into his mind that we were substantial fruit and potato growers – we never contradicted him. We knew enough to make remarks about hard times, reduced acreages, blight and marketing boards. In return he handed us tickets to fish the burgh waters for three days each. It was not corruption on inter-continental scale, for the total cost to his firm was only £12.

Knowing that there is no fishing on a Sunday in Scotland, we had timed our arrival for Monday morning. By the time our new best friend had given us a wholesome lunch we were ready to move to the Deveron. We were also ready to remove the bulk of our clothes, for the area was in the middle not only of a drought, but also a heatwave. The temperature on the hotel thermometer registered 68°. We made our way to the river in our hired car and were not all that surprised to find it little more than a trickle, running between high banks and substantial rocks.

The Deveron flows down, pretty slowly during a drought, from the Cabrach and through Huntly, where it is joined by the Bogie. The Bogie can be a fierce little river, but this March it looked like a spawning ground for small brown trout. The Deveron then marches, reinforced by a number of nameless burns, until it is supplemented not far upstream of Rothiemay, by the Isla. After that, even in low water, it is at least a river, passing between widely separate banks and making it clear to the imaginative what, with a little water in it, it could amount to.

It took Jack and me, in our shirtsleeves and barrier cream – we had come ready for any emergency – only that one afternoon to realise that we had come a long way for nothing. When we got back to our hotel and discovered the best of all malt whiskies, the local Glendronnach, we had the courage to invite our new friend for a conference of despair – for where were we going to spend the next two days? That question led to our meeting with Tom Tewnion (called for ever by Jack, who never mastered surnames, Tom Trinian).

Tom worked on the railways in between fishing. Even then, the shadow of Beeching was falling. The service was diminishing and Tom found himself with more fishing time – but eagerly watching his rail obligations to prevent any danger of premature redundancy. What he did not know about fishing the Deveron could be written with a thick nib on a twenty pence piece. He had fished the whole river with or without permission. He had become, without trying too hard, a local fishing legend.

He quickly took us in hand. With multiple Scottish oaths, he explained the hopelessness of the water we were fishing. 'It'll cost you £2 a day, but I'll take you to the Forbes Arms' water.' – and the next day we were meeting Frank Forbes of the Forbes Arms and then going down the brae to a greatly enlarged Deveron – until then I had thought that a brae was a bonny Scottish girl.

Oh that brae! Fit as we were, it was to become a daily ordeal – particularly the return journey; by the time we reached the top, the Deveron was a flat ribbon below our feet, our hearts were thumping and our muscles were aching. There was an alternative – a kind of spiral track to the hut at the bottom (a tiny hut, incidentally, on which someone had painted the deathless message 'Flood 16 foot. No fish in hut'). Once the car had been towed to the top again (£5 even in those days), we decided that it was better to run down the hill and fight our way back on foot. Some years later William and I had to make the journey twice because we could not carry all the fish in one go.

That first year, in the low water, even the fine Forbes Arms' pools, with such names as Corniehaugh, Sunny Brae and Woodend, were unlikely to provide us with much except kelts, but even those – tenderly returned – were a relevation to Jack and me.

The Deveron can provide fish from March onwards – but like all other rivers its spring run has deteriorated. From early summer the run increases and includes the large numbers of seatrout for which the river is most famous. We were fishing the Deveron before the disease struck and when the water was right – pale gold and dropping, after rains on the Cabrach. It provided fishing that was fantastic – plenty of seatrout averaging two pounds and more, grilse and some really big salmon. I was broken twice in Sunny Brae by big fish that went round rocks – and I was a much more competent fisherman by then. One of the great sights was to see Tom coming down the brae by the fence, rod over his shoulder, until at the river's edge, when, without pause, the first long slinky cast was delivered. We fished, on his instructions, with a pair of small flies – mostly Cinnamon and Gold and small silver Stoats' Tails – guaranteed to lure both seatrout and salmon. He guided our faltering steps into the paths of many fish, charmed our wives, who by that time were coming with us to the Forbes Arms (which must have been the best tiny fishing hotel in Scotland), and regaled us all with scurrilous stories in the bar in the evening.

One time we saw, fishing the opposite bank, a small man with a spinning rod. 'The bugger's got one on', Tom explained, as if mortally insulted. After twenty minutes while the little man stood like a statue, winding slowly, Tom said, 'The bugger's got no pressure on'. He ran like a stag upstream, to a place opposite. A great stream of Scottish invective poured across the river. The man bowed and went on winding. 'The bugger's foreign', shouted Tom, wading into the river at the one place where crossing was easy. He walked straight up to the fisherman, snatched the rod from his hand, adjusted the pressure on the reel, played and landed the fish – and without another word waded back to our side.

Tom was to fish with us for many more years and became a close and valued friend. It was a sad day when Jack telephoned me and told me that he had just heard that Tom Trinian had died.

The second and third time we went we took William with us, for the trout fishing. This was mid-April and the river was seething with free-rising trout. It was so good that we all abandoned our salmon rods (of salmon there was no sign), and spent our time catching brown trout up to two pounds. Inevitably a call from Will indicated that he had hooked a very big trout indeed. It certainly weighed eight pounds, and was a salmon, caught more by luck than judgement, on a size 12 Greenwell's Glory. All youngish boys catch eight pound salmon on size 12 Greenwell's Glories – but this was the time when a camera was in place and in the family album is a photograph of the most delighted person in the universe holding his fish in the air, with a look of total disbelief.

Because of her overwhelming powers, goodness and accomplishments, Marjorie sometimes becomes plural. 'We can't possibly decide', her family would say, 'without a word with them'. In particular, it was a certainty, that on the rare occasions when 'they' went away and left us, organised life, as we knew it, was bound to come to a halt.

At some moment in 1968 she decided that she should fly to Nebraska to see her mother. It turned out, a year later, to have been the last time she saw her alive, so it was a most fortunate decision. We, the survivors, quickly perceived it as a great reason to escape the chaos, by going on holiday together and staying at the Forbes Arms. William and I travelled with the fishing tackle in my fading blue Triumph 2000. Richard took the other car, a kind of Hillman Estate, together with his first travelling girlfriend; they were to leave us at the end of the week to collect the family's mainstay from Heathrow, in the unlikely event of all the flights working out safely. We all had a deep distrust of aircraft.

When we arrived, the Deveron was so low as to be only trout-fishable, but on the third day a thunderstorm on the Cabrach changed all that. The next morning it was running, high and brown. We fished worm but only caught a flounder – but on the next day it was sparkling along, eighteen inches above summer level, deep gold. We all raced down the brae that morning, three Scots from Glasgow with spinning rods,

William and I, the purists, cantering along with our fly rods. The only thing we were short of was time, because at about midday the pick-up, God willing, was taking place and she would be 'phoning me.

Cutting a record two hours fishing down to size, between us we caught three salmon, two grilse and four seatrout. It is a myth, of course, that in high water, big flies must inevitably be used. We caught all these on size 10 doubles and size 12 droppers. 'Class always tells', murmured William, when we heard that the spinners had drawn a blank.

Class had not told to the point of making provisions for such a catch. We had no bass bags, no plastic sacks. We had to make two heart-stopping ascents of the brae to get the booty to the car.

Opening the car boot at the Forbes Arms, slightly ostentatiously, a brown voice behind me said, 'Gee, what a catch'. I turned to look into the eyes of the first beautiful redhead I had ever seen. 'Are they salmon?' she asked (she was American I learned later, but not from Nebraska). Then – 'Would you possibly consider selling me one?' I pulled out a three pound seatrout. 'It's only a small salmon', I said, 'but you're very welcome to it, in return for a pint of beer, both for me and my son.'

While the beer was disappearing down our parched throats, the telephone rang. They were back. They were safe. They had been collected. As we packed and got ready to storm back to Cambridgeshire, a perfect day was complete.

The Deveron gave us a lot more joy, but always there was the fear of too little water – and it was a long way to go for no fishing at all. Just how dire water shortage could be, was demonstrated when Jack and I and our wives and two of Jack's friends booked ourselves into a lovely hotel at Lybster which had let to us a week on the Berriedale, half way up the north east coast of Scotland. I have often wondered since how good this marvellous, but distant, stream might be in high water. During our week, it was so low that the total flow would have taken time to fill a bucket. The Berriedale valley is one of Scotland's loveliest places, wooded, secluded, sweet-smelling, full of variety. Even when we were there we could see the potential. There were plenty of deep pools. In the clear water we could see the bored salmon lying in wait for rain. In one pool there was an enormous fish, forty pounds we called it, having never seen a real one. We floated flies over it. We cast sinking nymphs beside it. We tried enormous American dry flies at dusk – it never moved. It couldn't. It nearly filled the pool in which it lay – but it was beginning to dawn on us that big rivers alone could provide us with water we could fish, whatever the weather.

My last visit to the Deveron was suitably dramatic. Marjorie was attending a conference at the University of Aberdeen, and husbands were welcome. We shared uncomfortable students' bunks. On the first morning I escaped to the Deveron where I wangled myself a day ticket to fish just opposite where we had fished for so many years. As my fly moved gently towards the fence where Tom Tewnion had fished all those years before, it was taken with a great swirl. The fish, a bright red ten-pounder, hand-tailed in an impossible place, was carried back to the university in triumph – and even gained an honourable mention in the speeches at that night's convention dinner.

CHAPTER TEN

On to the Dee

Once we had survived the comparative disaster of the Berriedale it became inevitable that we faced facts and searched for places on those bigger rivers. Nobody but a fisherman would have counted the Berriedale week as a disaster. The hotel at Lybster was all and more than we had any right to expect. The valley of the little river was sheer delight – we were cheated by the total absence of good fishing days; we were also sustained by the Lybster golf course, nine informal holes, green fees paid to the Postmaster in the High Street.

I was doing my distant fishing with Jack Bridger. In America he would have been called, unselfconsciously, my buddy. We had much in common, in and out of the river; our wives were close friends; but though we had both climbed reasonably high on our respective work ladders, we were still prisoners of that holiday system that encases 95% of people of working age. Our short breaks were too precious to squander; the rewards of one on a good river might, we hoped, make it a bargain. Travelling and accommodation is much the same in good and bad ventures.

Among Marjorie's more endearing patients was Gina Maris, a tall, well-constructed blonde whose hair hung down her back like a gleaming waterfall – or that is how, fifteen years later, I like to remember it. Her husband was forging for himself, in a very big way, a place in North Sea oil; it was natural for them to move to the Aberdeen area. Move they did, to a nice modern 'Poppy Lodge' overlooking Deeside. As soon as I heard this I sent her a postcard, exhorting her to keep her eyes wide open for salmon fishing. It turned out to be a miraculously canny cast.

Just three weeks later the 'phone rang and Gina told me that she had met a gillie, Ian Anderson, who was in a position to offer a week's fishing on Upper Blackhall, at a price that could be thought about without faintness. It was as if she was offering us a cut-price ticket to paradise. Getting onto a good beat (even, as we were to discover, at the worst time) was a great achievement for people like Jack and me, without influential fishing friends. Good fishing, really good fishing, is mainly in the hands of an unassailable old boy network; or of letting agents to whom the biggest rent payer is the beau ideal; or, more creditably, of a succession of loyal people who take fishing year after year, in good times and in bad. When rods become available they expect consideration for their own friends. Had Gina been some kind of an agent, instead of an attractive lady whose only previous contact with salmon had been on fishmongers' slabs, she would have qualified for a tranche of commission. She was soon to show, delightfully, that she was piscatorially naive.

When we got together with Ian, we were able to arrange one lovely week each year in July for four years, full of pleasures and including one great adventure. I see from my fishing book that the four years produced twelve fish, which by my standards was totally satisfactory.

No fishing on the Aberdeenshire Dee can be less than perfect. It is a clean, clear, beautiful rocky river, tumbling down one of Europe's most magical valleys – even the names of the waters make the fingers tingle – Invercauld, Monaltrie, Dinnet, Ballogie, Crathies: what memories they invoke for those lucky enough to know them! You cannot possibly rate our big rivers in a kind of football league order. The Tay, no doubt, has its adherents; so, for sure, does the Spey; and certainly the Tweed. The Dee provides its owners and occupiers with pleasures that must seem to them paramount.

In the good old days, when the river was regarded as the prime early river in the UK (as it is by many now and with good reason), the fishing tended to stop in mid-June. Quiet descended on its banks, with no noise but the swish of the scythes of gillies who had little to do but keep away the flies and compete with one another in producing the best kept beat. The proprietors had had their triumphs, and nothing much happened until the back-end, when a run of fishermen in the upper beats would appear, catching the autumn salmon. Even so, the Dee being the river that it is, only a few selected cock-fish were killed and sent for smoking. The rest were gently returned.

Like the clarity of the water, the silver gleam of the Dee salmon has always been admired and cherished. During one of my July holidays I heard an exchange between the witty and urbane Esmond Drury and another rod at the hotel. The other rod had caught a mildly brown fish and had displayed it on the hotel plate. 'It's great to see men with independent minds', muttered the colonel, 'but surely we should have been shown that kipper after it had been smoked . . . or has it been already?'

Trying to save money that first year, we stayed at a fairly awful fast food hotel where they sang songs till midnight. There was also a fire warning after which we realised that we might easily have fried with the fast food. This gave added importance to the marvellous lunches our wives contrived for us in the fishing hut – a splendid one with cooking facilities, a stove to keep out the July cold and great piles of beautifully cut logs, prepared by Ian. We had no complaint about our sausage and chips hotel because you get what you pay for; but in subsequent years we moved to Banchory Lodge and to hell with the cost. The food was good, but best of all was the view from our bedroom window – of salmon leaping as they tried to make up their minds whether to travel up the main river or take their chance in the Feugh.

Upper Blackhall is a remarkably generous right-hand beat with fine holding pools and a cosy and stirring proximity to the waters of Cairnton, to which 'Jock Scott' in his book *Greased Line Fishing* gave world fame – not just to the waters but also to the technique (so new and original at the time) of greased line fishing as practised by the late A. H. E. Wood. We would look across to the house (or was it a bungalow?); it was not a bit difficult to see or imagine a sober-clad figure within, slowly preparing himself for one of his six-fish sorties.

Upper Blackhall is a great beat because it includes pools for high water fishing as well as low. A two-foot flood transforms the beat into an entirely different fishery – where one found oneself (guided by Ian) in places that had not seemed to exist in low water.

The low water fishing is kept afloat by the slap, the run of fish that enters the river during the weekend times when the nets are lifted. (The Dee's prospects – and value – have been increased recently by permanent lifting of most of the river nets.) Every Tuesday, Wednesday or Thursday, under almost any conditions, our hearts were warmed by the sight of bright jumping fish – some, not many – as they moved into, and out of, the beat. These were the ones that might be catchable, though each year the resident salmon kept us reasonably happy by their antics – and even occasionally surprised us by taking our fly.

The Dee, with the supplement of Ian Anderson's advice, helped to convert me into a bigger river fisherman. In low water, which is mostly all there ever is in mid-summer, it is not a huge river but its pools are deep and long, with plenty of places where the maximum cast came in useful. I had moved by then to a carbon fibre rod and was beginning to enjoy covering a lot of water. My fifteen-foot Walker, which has served me without complaint ever since, was one of the early ones and I for one was not aware of the potential danger of these rods. Nor, very sadly, was one of the Dee's best loved gillies who touched a live wire with one and was electrocuted. Ian nearly killed himself as well, dragging the unfortunate man away from the flying volts.

The hut at Feragh is the heart of Upper Blackhall, overlooking the beautiful pool. One morning, at five o'clock, when Jack and I had let our enthusiasm get the better of us, we watched two otters playing among the rocks at the run-in. From the hut we could watch the pool, recoup our energy, spot new fish. The same sister who had been with us during the dramatic week at Holne Chase came and joined us one summer. We never cured her of her particular way of referring to the hut. 'Are we eating lunch in the shed today?' she would ask.

Gina came and joined us for lunch in 'the shed' and was fascinated by the fish she saw. It seemed to her that salmon fishing was like roach fishing, but on a larger scale. Throw a line at a fish and it would be yours, was her idea. I asked her to come down to the pool and catch one. She readily agreed. We walked to the edge of the water – I in my waders, she in jeans. 'I'll take off my trousers', she said and before I could faint they were in a heap on the stones. She had on a bikini underneath and must have been nearer to a dryad than anything recently seen in those sacred waters. For fifteen minutes she tried to cast over a friendly fish, but in the end gave it up.

Then in 1978 we had the water we had craved. Two nights' and days' rain produced a two-foot rise in the Dee. We were left with three days to fish the dropping river in the new pools to which Ian had introduced us. There was a big influx of fish, showing all over the place, but our joint catch was two salmon and three seatrout. It was very nearly much bigger.

One morning I went ahead of Jack to fish the tail of Moral, our top pool. The river was sweeping out of the pool in a V-shaped glide towards the other bank. It was a difficult spot to fish from our side – yet the angles were right. I had to slide down a perpendicular bank to get into the water, but the problems of landing a fish did not worry me. I knew that Jack was fishing close behind me and we had agreed to meet quite quickly in case of emergencies.

The emergency arose when I cast over a fish that showed in the glide, one that was entering the tail of the pool. It was a memorable cast, a once in a lifetime thirty-five yarder, performed as all the best things are, without effort. When the fish took, I tightened with a calmness that would have surprised all my friends. As if inspired (or in a trance) I played this fish for ten or fifteen minutes. It cruised around the pool as though I were not there, but luckily never tried to return to sea. Ten minutes later, when I was putting on some real pressure, I caught my first glimpse of him. My knees wobbled. He was huge, the fish I had never thought I would catch. No sign of Jack, though I had been shouting loudly – and then the fish was lying in front of me, not on his side, but very nearly static. I guided him into the bank, bent down to grab his tail and failed to hold it. It was so thick that I could not get a grip on it. That produced another long and frightening run, but this time he came back more quickly. Nowadays I would somehow or other have got my fingers into his gills. Then, all I could do was have another shot at his tail. I feasted my eyes at his huge depth, bronze in the coloured water, then, as I turned him towards me, saw the hook come out.

Ten minutes later Jack arrived to find me sitting, stunned, on the bank. Buddies do not make angry noises. All I said was, 'Where the hell have you been?' I found out later that he had been lying in the ferns, a hundred yards downstream, exchanging sweet nothings with a wife whom he still insisted on calling Sweetheart. Fishing the other bank was Philip Green, whom we called the Dee Otter. He is a man of few words and good advice. 'Anyone who fishes this river, where there are always big fish, without a gaff in his pocket for emergencies like yours, doesn't deserve success'. I still decide not to carry a gaff, but understand with feeling what he meant.

CHAPTER ELEVEN

Getting There

One of the excitements of going fishing, it must be conceded, is getting there – and back, too. The return journey has its own attractions, with the post of a week or two neatly piled in the kitchen, the possibility of a premium bond win that will pay for the holiday – and all the developments in the garden at a time when two weeks can turn buds into flowers, and flowers into small green tomatoes.

We are easy travellers. We would be in any first team for which selection is made on the basis of smooth early starts. We have a treasured small alarm clock. I won it at golf on a day, many years ago, when the ball flew straight and true – and there were ten prizes for the twelve competitors. We set it for 3.30 or 4.30 a.m. but, whatever the time, we have not yet heard the alarm. We always wake up from restless sleep before it goes off.

The car will have been loaded the night before, except for the final suitcase. No one is a finer organiser of a loaded car than Marjorie. Things get stowed neatly away; nothing is left out. I, on the other hand, make helpless noises like, 'Have you put in an extra sweater?' or, 'What are we going to do about money?' My fishing tackle is kept in a stout wooden box. By the time I have checked it half a dozen times, it is certain that nothing has been forgotten. The rods and the waders are added to the pile in the hall and they also get stowed neatly away.

While she is packing the final suitcase I go and make tea, so sweet and strong that it is a meal on its own. With this safely

Our wedding day. Outside the church at Detmold.

Waiting for a rise on the Itchen, 1946.

The first salmon. William Barr on the Deveron.

Marjorie, my gillie, on honeymoon in the Trossachs.

Sylvie Tissier, Marjorie and me on a seat beside Carron;
Crocus and Jasmine flat out as usual.

Sylvie fishing the run at Carron Bridge.
Both photos © Sylvie Tissier.

Winter repair work on the Babingley.

A flooded Yorkshire Esk at Egton Bridge.

Jack Bridger.

John Norman with a September fish from the Dee.

Fishing the Bruton Run; tide at the perfect level.

D. Barr on Henry's Fork, the Snake River, Idaho.

Fishing with a guide at Harriman's Ranch.

A Spey grilse from Carron.

D. Barr fishing the Duck Decoy, River Babingley.

inside us (gunfire we called it in the army) we will be dressed and away within minutes. Hardly ten words will have passed between us and only the dogs, noticing their much restricted space, will have shown any traces of early-morning grumpiness. Almost inevitably (after all her organisation), Marjorie will ask – when we are a mile or so on our way – 'Do make sure I've got my handbag'. That voluminous black creature will contain our money, cheque books, pills, unanswered letters and telephone numbers. Its absence would make life very difficult indeed.

The changes have been dramatic – to cars in particular. Our journeys to Holne Chase were made in ten or twelve horsepower cars (they did not know about c.c. in those days) that had been bought second-hand without warranty. There were children as well as dogs, and space was precious. We even had to resort to roping luggage on top of the roof, covering it with black plastic so that it looked like a woefully swollen mobile wen. We never had any breakdowns more lethal than a puncture, but the 320-mile journeys were very hard work. We could not average as many miles in an hour as forty; thirty-five was a cause for a certain smugness. There were no motorways. We went through towns rather than round them, and there was no defined best route. The AA sent us little booklets showing how to get there with encouraging notes like 'Here you will be passing through a well wooded valley beside a little river' – but even their advice varied from year to year. Meantime we were seeing England's little towns – Ilminster, Ilchester, and even Yeovil – that we shall probably never see again. We arrived, totally exhausted, in time for an evening meal, having put up with two hours of, 'Are we nearly there, Daddy?' as the boys, too, ran out of patience.

There were no roadside Happy Eaters or Little Chefs. The picnic was the day's best break. If we wanted to call for a coffee, the only places were the lorry drivers' pull-ins, if we were lucky enough to find one. Lorry drivers, being tough and independent, demanded and got excellent food and drink, and so did we travelling families. One morning we made a five o'clock start back to Cambridgeshire, relying on finding breakfast on the way. We found nothing to sustain us – or our good nature – until we were on the Northampton side of Oxford. It had been a week when there had been no water, no fish, and unremittingly icy winds. Morale was pretty low by the time the eggs and bacon arrived, at midday. The family photographs taken at that time show strains and stresses that driving troubles did not explain. We were both working full time and under full pressure. Money and spare time seemed short.

The journeys to Scotland have been, of course, the big ones; not only because the fishing hopes were so high, but because we were hastening to what had become favourite places. By this time, for various reasons, the boys were not always with us. Up the old A.1 we went, with few towns bypassed and no dual carriageway to speak of. We never even considered doing the 500-mile journey in one great dash. We spent the night in various places in the Border Country, immaculate little private hotels kept by immaculate and thrifty lowland Scots, where lineoleum shone like mahogany, the baths looked as though they had never been used, and an under-employed husband would lurk, helpfully, in the background.

With the vast road improvements to the A.1 and the A.9 in particular, cutting out the halfway stop became more simple. The A.9 had been the chief barrier, too narrow and primitive to overtake the lines of hastening caravans. Now it is modern, straight and reasonably fast; an arrow through some of the most fantastic remote mountain country in the British Isles. Everyone should, if they possibly can, take, at least once, the journey from the area of Aviemore, past Dalwhinnie and down to Tayside, when the sun is starting to rise on a fine August morning, the heather blancmange pink, the granite rosy, the willow herb in full bloom and the sky technicoloured.

We have got into the habit of the one-day dash. We permute the various routes in search of the easiest. All the way up the A.1, with the bait of the coastal road to Edinburgh beyond Berwick – or hard left at Scotch Corner, across the narrow waist of England to Penrith, then north to Perth via Sterling, motorway or fast dual carriageway all the time (except through Dunblane, that worthy township with its Staki's Hydro, which is in the process of being bypassed). Whatever route we take to Speyside there are seldom more than twenty extra miles in it – nor are there if we are going through Inverness to Ullapool (stepping off point, thanks to Mr. MacBrayne, to the Islands; or, as lately, a holiday place in its own right). The only destination that I would not try to reach in one journey, nowadays, is the very North. The east coast road reminds me of the A.9 in the old days and it takes a glowing prospect (like Lord Thurso's Thurso at its very best) to lure us there. Just recently the effect of the flying years, and of waning energies and ambitions has made us a little less keen on the 500-mile effort. The halfway stop, in the more than half-decent hotels we have started to pinpoint within fifty miles or so south of Edinburgh, is becoming something to look forward to.

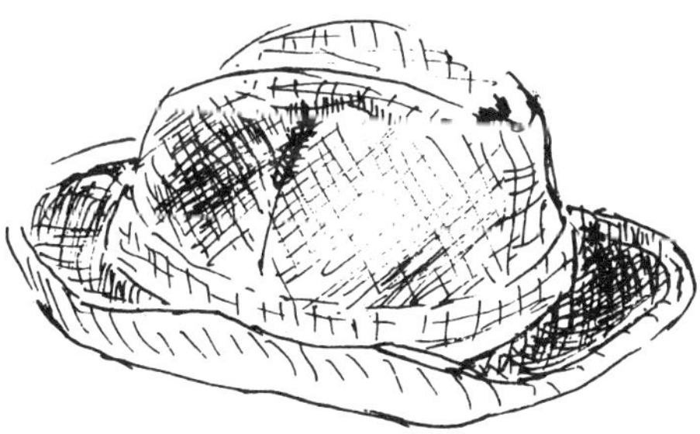

CHAPTER TWELVE

The Spey. At Last!

For some time my busy little mind had been contemplating bigger and even more exciting rivers, if such existed – and if they did, wondering if they would ever become available? From time to time we had passed over the Spey at Grantown, but it had not looked all that irresistible. One of the delights of this river, that we were later to discover, is that it carefully conceals its secrets and only reveals them to those who wade and fish it. Besides, an uninformed friend had told me that it was a spinning river. All you had to do was cast as far across as possible, let the current swing the spinner back to your bank, wind in and start all over again. No more scurrilous tale could have been told about Scotland's finest fly water.

One Christmas during a party with some friends near Cambridge, our hosts started to show us movies of their last holiday. Normally this is the moment when I flee like a ferret, but we were all fishermen and these were going to be pictures of the Spey at Craigellachie. There they were, Dick, Hugh and Alan, striding about this massive river, standing in the middle with the water racing by them, wading sticks tilted forward like extra legs. And they were landing fish – gleaming beauties from the golden water. It was, for me, love at first sight. Filled with the good Haddenham wine, I telephoned that night (29th December I see from my diary) and booked us a double room and a week's fishing in the third week in April. The lady at the other end seemed in no way surprised. The hotel, at the time, controlled all the fishing.

Snow was falling on the night I made the reservation and

was falling again on that bleak April day when we started out on our first Spey week. We could hardly know (though we might have guessed) that during the next dozen years we would become familiar with every mile and every permutation of the route, normally doing the 500 miles in one dash, driving in turns an hour and a half each. Later, too, diminishing mortgages and an increased income produced for us quicker and more comfortable cars. During that first long journey, however, we held our breath and hoped that the banger would keep banging. Hardly averaging forty miles an hour, we found dinner, bed and breakfast, well short of the border, taking off for the A.9, duly refreshed, the next morning. The snow had long since turned to driving rain, the roads were flooded, the fields had standing water; below the snowcaps of Aviemore we could see the silver streaks of falling water. The Spey was brown and enormous, over its banks in many places. Not very good for wading, I thought nervously. Marjorie, by this time was driving – having realised for many years that my habit of driving and examining rivers simultaneously would one day certainly be fatal. The meanest bookie would have given long odds against any of the hotel's eight rods catching, or seeing, a fish.

It was, predictably, a long, dull, cold week, casting heavily leaded spinners into a flat, featureless river, surging towards the sea. Whenever the river showed signs of dropping and revealing its secrets, down came the rain again. It is unfair to judge the act of spinning by this hopeless experience, but my spinning career was getting nearer and nearer to its death and this was another nail in its coffin. We all gathered together in the bar each night (with the saddened parties who were fishing the really expensive beats in the area) and decreased the stocks of Macalan.

The real victory of the week was the chance to make the acquaintance of the hotel – huge, warm, friendly and generous – and of Margaret Garrow, the manageress, one of the greats; warm, friendly, generous and very Scottish. Running a fishing hotel can never be a sinecure. Half the fishermen are almost certain to be frustrated or disgruntled. At least half the wives will be the same – and probably bored as well. Margaret presided over us all like an attractive and tolerant head mistress. She told me, almost sadly, that I had no hope of any kind of getting a rod in July (grilse time, apart from everything else) this year or next. She was booked up solidly this year and the next at all the good times, and very few changed their minds – because, once out of her fishing family, they had to go to the bottom of the queue if they ever hoped to return. We regarded our week as a taste of how roughly life can treat the deserving – and as an opportunity to start edging our feet under the hotel table. We were even allowed to book for April in the following year.

Coming out of Ha'penny Lane (where our house is) at the end of the following June, I took the corner onto the fairly main road to Friday Bridge and March with more than the usual care. Traffic appears at full tilt and without warning from behind the Church Hall. One moment the road is empty; the next, thirty tons thunder by, almost taking the skin off your nose. that day, I drove along with concentration centred on the danger zone, eyes stiffly turned right as though a Major General stood there – then *crash*. I had run straight into a car parked on the corner on my side; such a possibility had never crossed my mind. Both cars were in a mess but at least I had the benefit of an insurance policy that provided me with a hired car whilst repairs were being done. I did not think the liability worth arguing about. A tiny plan, in fact, was beginning to take shape. The next week Marjorie was going on a five day cytology course. It was going to be very grim indeed for the one they left behind. That evening I made two telephone calls. The first was to Margaret Garrow. I reminded her that I was one of the most charming of her new best friends. Luckily she had enjoyed one or two of my articles. 'I certainly remember you, Mister Barr', she somehow made the Mister Barr sound rhythmic, with a highland lilt. I told her that I had been wondering, a little feverishly, whether she had a spare rod during the coming week. There was a long, long pause – 'I believe that someone up there is keeping an eye on you, Mister Barr'. That morning it seemed, one of the regulars had telephoned to say he had 'flu and could not make the journey. Within an hour the Garrow grapevine had revealed that the wretch had booked into another hotel and would be fishing Knockando. 'He won't be fishing here again', continued this angel, 'so you may as well take his rod – do you want a single or a double room?'

Two minutes later, mouth dry, hand shaking, I was talking to the General Accident at Perth. Scotland had evidently declared a love-and-honour D. Barr day. 'Yes, they would have a fine clean car waiting for me at Aberdeen station on Sunday night.' 'Yes, it would be grand if I would leave it there the next Sunday and hand in the keys to the hire firm.' All that could now thwart me was an earthquake, a revolution, a train accident, a cloud burst – or a dire attack of 'flu. Everything turned out to be bright and beautiful.

I have already touched on the time 'they' left us to go and see mother, leaving us free to empty the Deveron. Now here 'they' were off again. It gives a ridiculously wrong impression. In all the years of marriage I doubt whether we have spent six weeks apart. (Once I went alone to join a party fishing the Spey's Carron beat. Even though the fishing was good. I grew so homesick that I came tearing home on the Thursday. My fishing friends either derided me or believed that there was an undefined but dishonourable reason.) On this first Spey July we were neither of us at a disadvantage. We would have been separated even if I had stayed at home.

The Craigellachie Hotel fishing must now be described. It is not, as will become clear, the hotel fishing any more, but that is what it is still called. It starts near the Aberlour sewage farm (could anything be more savoury?), with a long pool recently named Campbells. It is a spinning high water pool, but I have had a couple out of it in the evenings on fly in lowish water. A quarter of a mile downstream the whole of the Spey roars through a narrow funnel into Broom Island. There are several fly taking places here, where fish lie, waiting to run upstream. Next, the 600 yards of Lower Broom Island where Alan Blower (if no one else) finds extraordinarily undetectable places to catch fish in high water. Then, the Garden Pool. Not easy to fish from our right bank – without being a silhouette – but always holding fish. We have a saying that we repeat each time we fish it. 'There's always a chance of a fish in the Garden Pool.' It is not a very nice pool. Next, The Rocks. I had hoped it would be called Barr's Rocks, because I was the first to bother to fish it (and catch one). Now everyone does and it is a recognised series of taking places. Then there is Sham-prach, a 400-yard long pool, capable of producing some very happy surprises. Hard work too. To fish it conscientiously takes a full hour, but it can be rewarding. Finally (on the top beat), Upper Tunnel Pool. The Spey curls round a very deep pool (down which it is rumoured that the enthusiastic men of Aberlour dropped a large brass cannon with German connections in 1939) to the beginning of the Lower Beat. Upper Tunnel fishes best from the left (or Easter Elchies) side, but fish are caught from time to time from the Craigellachie bank. There is an insidious approach, very fast, very shallow, very easy to cast the fly which gets further and further into the pool – to the points where the Tunnel salmon show increasingly temptingly. When the fisherman has reached what he judges to be the last point of safety, he turns round and finds that it is very, very nearly impossible to wade back into the teeth of the current, shallow or not. Many a good man has worked his way back with more than a tinge of fear; the return journey always takes up unpredicted minutes. It is a place to watch with care.

That should be the end of the top beat, but it is not. The

next stop is the Boat Pool at the most downstream end of the Craigellachie fishing. A fine pool this, usually allocated to the top beat, on the basis that there is so much fishing between Lower Tunnel Pool and the top of the Boat Pool, that it is only fair to allocate it to the upstream beat. It takes newcomers a number of years to understand this fishing folly, but no one ever wants to change the system.

At the top end of the lower beat is the Lower Tunnel Pool, a spinning pool only, except in the lowest water when a reasonably brave fisherman can fish the glide at the tail with success. Below this there is at least half a mile of good fly fishing water – Upper Slabs, Lower Slabs, Lower Lower Slabs, then a long unnamed stretch with plenty of lies that leads into the Doo's Nest (a remarkably prolific pool when times are good) and finally into the Bridge Pool which at present has become silted up and is not as good as it was – though it can be very good in high water. This is the pool over which the famous Telford Bridge holds elegant sway and from which all manner of holidaymakers watch the casting fishermen below, hoping against hope to see some action. There is another pool, Shanks, between Bridge and Boat, but it fishes badly from the hotel bank and you have to be a mountain goat to fish it.

Altogether the two beats cover two and a half miles of water – and each year the catch is in the region of 400 fish. Those of us who have suffered in the spring at Craigellachie, when fish have been few and far between, and when the tenants of such beats as Delfur, Rothies and Arndilly have come in each evening with heavy sacks which they removed with modesty from the boots of their land rovers, realise that this is not Scotland's best piece of fishing – but it gives fun and satisfaction to many people to whom rents on other beats would be prohibitive. When the water is high at Craigellachie (and our catches very limited) we nod our heads and say knowingly, 'Of course this is essentially a low water beat'. When the water is low and we are still not in the money we murmur, equally knowingly, 'What we want is another foot of water'. Traditionally we judge the water level by the number of stones showing on the Telford Bridge. I once received a deserved Scottish rebuke for calling them bricks. In the hotel rod room is a black and white photograph showing the bricks we count. There were eleven that day, just right.

In this short summary of the hotel water, the Doo's Nest deserves a few more words. The Doo no longer nests there, but the lie remains close to the cliff round which the Spey races. The water is not deep, but to fish it with a fly it is necessary to wade right out to it. So swift is the current that it is all one can do to stand up in the fastest parts and to shift one's balance for the cast. There is always one moment of total apprehension, when the sand and the stones are slithering from beneath your boots and the eighteen inches of current has built up to somewhere near your shoulder blades when you say, 'Whatever am I doing this for? Certainly not for fun.' Then a yard further down the current abates and it all seems more sensible. I once had four fish on (not all landed) in four consecutive visits to the Doo's Nest – so it is not as silly as it sounds. When I was younger I called it my favourite salmon pool. Now there are one or two others I prefer.

I started to catch Spey salmon on that solo week in July, after the car accident. I think I caught five. The river was high (so much for the low water beat theory), and I had never before caught big fish in a fast swollen river. Each one made me think that the fly had caught a tiger and each one, straight from the sea, was a treasure. How I managed to get them from Aberdeen station to Peterborough (where my wife met me as though I was a returning hero), I shall never know.

CHAPTER THIRTEEN

Craigellachie, Next Bite

Fate and good fortune must have been trotting along beside us.

First of all Dick, Alan and Hugh asked me to join them in their regular April week – called their 'No Fish Week'. Then I managed to get a second rod in the July week enabling me to include Jack Bridger in this magic circle. I do not remember how much extra we paid the hotel for the fishing, but it was quite a nominal amount. In retrospect and with lots of hindsight, everything one paid in the past seems small, but even at the time it seemed good value. I could write a full chapter on the charms and virtues of Margaret Garrow, who did so much for us all – but the career of a lady like her could not be expected to stop at even such a place as Craigellachie. Once she moved into the five star circuit, the future of the hotel and its fishing, though we did not know it, was in the melting pot. In happy ignorance, we busily pursued our Scottish fish.

The April 'No Fish Week' became increasingly desirable as the four wives got to know each other better. They, too, built up their Speyside lives, walking down the railway line in the mornings to Aberlour to have their hair done, moving with glee to Elspeth's Boutique in Rothes which, they said, would leave most southern equivalents breathless. I know that Marjorie bought a coral frock there that gave her active service for at least five years – and me many great pleasures. Then off they would go to the flesh pots of Elgin, Inverness and Grantown, buying what they could easily have got at home, but returning with eyes sparkling with pleasure, as if they had found a brand new North Pole or won a parcel of Premium Bond prizes. Our family ownership of Pringle sweaters and Viyella shirts used to soar every April; the stock has been on the wane since the end of the April fishing parties – in spite of the fact that Robert Goddard of Wisbech has always had the whole collection available from February onwards.

At the start, the 'No Fish Weeks' were not as bad as they sounded. Usually we caught three or four between us, sometimes more, occasionally fewer. One of the more memorable moments was catching a ten-pounder at the run-in to Broom Island and then sitting on a stone by the river's edge, thinking how clever I had been, and listening on a portable radio to the Cup Final and hearing Ipswich Town's winning goal scored. The voice seemed to come from another planet. Then, another April, when I was involved in editing *The Haig Guide to Salmon Fishing in Scotland*, two of the publishers came for a couple of nights to get the feel of the problem. One, an ace photographer, followed me for an hour on the first morning. Stunned by the fact that nothing was being caught, he wandered upstream to take some shots of the view, and returned twenty minutes later just as I landed my only fish of the week. So much for the action pictures.

When you first cross the Spey on the A.9 it is, in normal weather, a small serene lagoon, yet in the next forty miles, joined by a hundred springs and burns and two major rivers, the Dulnain and the Avon, it becomes massive and powerful even at low summer level. It is a golden river, passing mainly over brown stones and rocks and at a speed that keeps them clean and smooth. All the time the salmon are moving in, in twos and threes, and creeping up the river, giving an occasional hooray as they swim to another pool. There are people who say how much more attractive than the Spey is this river or that; but with its pleasant banks, its stands of broad leafed trees and its lines of bushes, it is my ideal river – and all the time there is the sudden depth, the unpredicted underwater obstruction, the huge rock that may overturn at a touch, that gives its friendliness just the hint of menace.

The Craigellache fishing has never been fly only, unlike much of the cream of the Spey fishing. The hotel rods have always tended to be disliked by the Easter Elchies fishermen on the other bank who have a fly only rule – and some difficult stretches where they can only Spey cast. Their side frequently gets bombed by spinners launched from the hotel bank. I have this feeling that if someone is spinning in front of you, your chances of a fish on the fly diminish, but I dare say that there are many stories that tell a contrary tale. I know I once caught a fish within seconds of a canoe going over its lie. By getting four rods together, we made sure that we did not aggravate ourselves or our friends opposite, as we were all fly fishermen. People tend to worry, if the water is high and even coloured, that the fly becomes hopeless. It probably will be if only the low water lies are fished, but (as on the Dee) it is possible to find places where a fly will succeed in these conditions. Similarly, if the water is cold (below the magic figure of 42°), then a larger fly and a sunk line will give nearly as good a chance as a spinner would, in a comparatively shallow river like the Spey – and will be more interesting to fish. I suppose the good adaptable fishermen (the ones that catch more fish than the rest) are the ones that go out ready for any eventuality carrying both spinners and fly fishing tackle. It is a topic that creates all kinds of strong emotions. The option of a single rod, with all my oddments in one pocket, is the one that appeals to my idle nature.

Jack Bridger was a patient and very persevering fisherman. He would certainly, occasionally, take a spinning rod with him – in fact I remember him, at a particularly blank time, catching, on a minnow, a fifteen-pounder in the lower end of the Tunnel Pool. When he arrived at where I was fishing a quarter of a mile downstream, carrying this beautiful fish, I paused to wonder, just for a moment, how much it would cost to rush to the car, speed to the tackle shop at Aberlour and equip myself with spinning rod, reel and minnows. So much for high principles. In the end I carried on with normal casting.

Jack did once have an unpleasant experience, though perhaps someone else should tell the story. We were fishing the Boat Pool together. The feature of the Boat Pool, we thought at the time, was the taking place at the head of the pool. Since then, over the years, we have found two other taking places below, but this was the only one we knew of then. The Boat Pool is a big pool, even by Spey standards. The river comes swiftly in at the head, slanting towards the other bank, beside which it runs, forming a deep eddy on our (hotel) bank. Halfway down it straightens itself out and courses more smoothly down to the next beat (Upper Arndilly). Because of the depth of the eddy it is difficult to fish the fast run – except at the top where our taking place is. It is possible, with care, to wade nearly half way over; but the bottom has been forged in hell. It is difficult, having found a home for one boot, to fit the other in without doing the splits. The procedure is to wade out as far as possible – and then cast towards the other bank – easing downstream a foot at a time between casts. Probably no more than ten casts need be involved, after which there is nothing to do but edge timidly back to the bank. That morning Jack, having developed some witty theory of his own said, 'You go first'. Normally we would toss. I crawled in like an unathletic frog and on my fifth cast the line started running off my reel. Getting back to land, playing a fish, is hairy, but once on shore landing it is simple, downstream through the big eddy and then up the sandy bank. As I pulled mine in (seven pounds) a fish rose in the taking place. 'My turn', said Jack moving in more swiftly than was safe. I watched him cast six, seven, eight and twelve times and muttered to myself that he was overdoing it. 'The fish went through', Jack grunted sitting down on a rock and letting me in. Having made the foul journey again, I hooked my second one on the very first cast. It was a ten-pounder. When I changed places with my fishing mate, I felt that I had already had more than a fair day's fishing. Jack's approach was now feverish. He crossed the underwater mountain tops as if they were flat and started to flail the water. Very relaxed indeed I watched him moving down into the eddy till it was nearly up to his neck. 'Not a fish in the pool', he growled, handing over the space to me,' you've had them all'. My next journey produced a thirteen-pounder and it marked a record morning and almost the end of a beautiful friendship – for though he fished the lie three more times, Jack never even had a pull.

There is a twist to this tale. The night before, the girls in the hotel office had told us that they were getting together to buy a fish to smoke. I thought it was sad that in a hotel where fishermen from all beats were bringing in their catches daily, nobody gave just one to these nice ladies. Big hearted Barr then opened his mouth a bit too wide. 'If I get one over twelve pounds tomorrow', said this magnanimous idiot, 'you shall have it.' I had not caught one over twelve pounds for four years and this was summer salmon time when they were bright and small. I was at least as good as my word when I handed over my thirteen pounder, and for a short time became the hotel's most popular guest. Two months later, immaculately packed, there arrived at home a pound of the most beautiful sliced smoked salmon I have ever had, 'From Meg & Co'.

The early halcyon days at the Craigellachie Hotel were on the wane. The successor, whom Margaret had trained and left behind her, had also moved and the owner was beginning to find her beloved hotel a growing headache. Rumours abounded – closing down – sold for millions to a German syndicate – leased to a group of Americans. The news broke in the winter.

It had indeed been sold, to a company said to be involved in the sale of fishing time-shares. The next thing that happened to us was an offer of our April week and also of the first week in August, take it or leave it, £8,500 each for the pair of weeks. After a mildly panic-stricken meeting, three out of four of us, plus a valued mutual friend, made the leap. One never knows details of other people's finances, but as far as the Barrs were concerned, it involved the sale of a large part of our savings. 'Of course we go ahead', Marjorie said, 'you'd be an idiot to lose the fishing – and where would you find any other? I'll borrow the lot if necessary'. So ahead we went. The 'No Fish Week' has behaved since, in perfect character, as the spring run diminishes. We all believe it will return. The August week has not yet reached the peaks of some of the July weeks, but has not been bad at all. The value of our investment has increased and the hotel, after various vicissitudes, was taken over by a very nice and very enthusiastic family (and more recently, sad to say, by a large hotel group).

I mentioned the halcyon days but omitted one particular element of pleasure. We managed to tie in the Dee week with the Craigellachie July week. Sometimes both worked. Never did both fail. The Barrs and the Bridgers would set forth from the Fens with the certainty of some great fishing. Crossing the great divide between Deeside and Speyside (on change-over Sunday), we started the habit of calling in at the golf club at Nethy Bridge. Success has manifested itself here in later years, in the shape of a new club house. When we were going there regularly, the club house was made of corrugated iron and looked like nothing so much as the economically built home of an obscure religious sect. No people ever got a warmer welcome at a golf club than we did. They had an honorary dispatcher called Bobby Ames, a delightful lady who gave us the feeling that she had been waiting for us all morning. She took our green fees with an apology (£1 each at weekends), and made sure we had a clear run from the first tee and came back, after nine holes, to cold drinks and sandwiches. Marjorie would be the last person to claim to be a classic golfer; she tends to count her shots in units of six and claims to have done a hole in three if she gets down in eighteen. It was at Nethy Bridge that she did her famous golf shot. Before a crowd of Scots, mostly small fry with single figure handicaps, she hit her drive almost out of sight – to within ten yards of the 240-yard distant green. It has never happened again, but I feel sure that it is still a topic of conversation there. Incidentally, the fourth and the last time we were able to combine the Dee-Spey double with the Nethy Bridge bonus, Bobby looked up as we came in and complained 'Where ever have you been dawdling? You're half an hour late!'

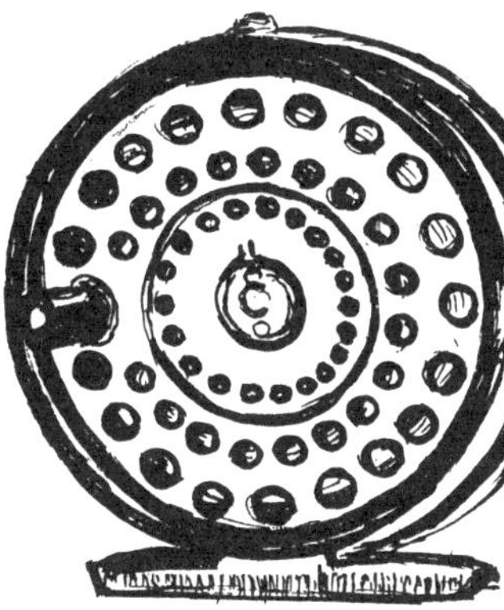

CHAPTER FOURTEEN

Foreign Parts

To soothe the shocked family in Nebraska, after they learned of our marriage, I had promised to go over for inspection as soon as could be managed. It took two years to establish the possibility of being three weeks away from the job. £350 a year did not produce the money such a journey would cost. Nor was three weeks any too long. Flying the Atlantic, it seemed to me then, was a job that conjured names like Lindbergh and Amelia Earhart; the ocean liners were still crammed with non-aviators. Fortunately, in more prosperous pre-David days, Marjorie had saved some of her earnings – which we used to finance the boat and 'plane journey to the west. Almost unnoticed, the first of the new generation had arrived (I was drunk on the night of his arrival). We had a year-old first born to bring with us, at no extra cost. Whatever my mystified mother-in-law might think of me, he was going to steal the grandmotherly heart.

We set out in the *Queen Mary*, tourist class (the lowest of the three), in a cabin filled with the flowers and telegrams with which the intrepid voyagers were smothered in those days. I seemed to sniff a whiff of the sinking of the *Titanic* and felt that the cheers of those lined up on the dockside as we floated away, seemed to bid farewell to those on a dangerous mission. Nothing untoward happened – except that our floating city bounced up and down on the heaving Atlantic. The member of the Island Race lost his appetite for what must have been the best eating opportunities since 1939. The girl from the prairies had to go slow for fear of putting on too much weight.

We were met in New York by a pair of Swedish/American

doctors who drove us to the airport. They were convinced that we would be close to starvation and fed us from a basket of hot dogs and hamburgers and, with time in hand, gave us a quick run over New York's bridges – typical American warmth. We had a ferocious ride in a Dakota, calling at Chicago, Des Moines, Omaha and Lincoln. If the sea had been rough it would have been a millpond compared to the air through which our twin-engined machine drove us. We held hands tightly, hers dry, mine wet with sweat, and swore never to fly again. She had borrowed a flowery hat for the arrival ceremony (hats were being worn then in Nebraska), but had to leave it in the 'plane, Richard having been very sick into it as we landed.

My previous view of the United States had been an exotic one, in 1939, spending Aunt Ada's £150 legacy. It had been two weeks of dances at Oyster Bay, suppers at The Stork Club, glorious girls with glorious accents, days and nights on the choicest parts of Long Island. The first sight of Nebraska was very different – though I came linked to an even more glorious girl with an even more delicious accent. Life in Scottsbluff was lived on a very different plane to that which I had known in 1939. Drinks were taken surreptitously, if at all. The various churches (mostly fiercely at odds with one another) were filled every Sunday. They even talked me into going. The whole area was hot, dry and heavily convention-bound. The precious days dragged by. This, incidentally turned out to be a very superficial first impression: over the years I have come to look on that part of the world as a sort of rarely visited second home, full of friendly and very nice people. Most of the happy hours were to be found at the family's Sow's Ear Ranch where, in the River Platte, which ran through it, and in a well filled gravel pit, I discovered some hard fighting carp in the ten pound bracket. They proved to be unable to resist the English ground baiting techniques. It should be added that the name of the ranch was directly connected with the Silk Purse that Dick, my brother-in-law, said that it could never become. He was over-modest; it was a lovely and enviable place. If it failed to produce an annual fortune, the reason was that Dick valued many other activities higher than the pursuit of dollars.

I had been promised – and got – a three-day round trip into Wyoming, to the Rocky Mountain foothills. In anticipation I had brought with me my fly rod and tackle. This was the first of my genuine foreign parts fishing and it exceeded every expectation.

We drove into the mountains through the kind of rolling grass cattle country that you see in Westerns (and so it should have been, because many of them are filmed in just such places). Leaving the paved roads, we drove upwards through intoxicating pine smells, and finally along winding tracks that even the mighty Pontiacs and Studebakers found taxing. In nearby grassland not only deer, but also antelope were playing. At about 7,000 feet we arrived at a large sheltered log-cabin, fifteen miles from where we had left the last hard road, in the centre of a small valley through which flowed the clear and spritely Cottonwood Creek, curling round the cabin like a letter C.

The Americans do things in style when they camp out. The entire first evening was spent unloading, carrying, making up the bunk beds, taking in the steaks and various liquid supplies. Later, before we went to bed, there was a display of a number of awesome collections of fishing tackle, mostly, to my surprise, spinning tackle, brightly coloured plastic rods and boxes of every conceivable kind of flasher, spoon, spinner and plug. There was a fly rod or two, but the flies looked ripe for fishing for salmon in coloured water. The big laugh was when I unfolded my modest wallet, twenty or so dry flies, 14's and 16's – Blue Duns, Olives, Tups, and other relics of the Test. 'No, Dave', they said with broad grins, 'our American trout are real greedy and like something solid to strike at.'

Something about the creek itself. It tumbled through rocky pool after rocky pool, a mile of it at least before it disappeared suddenly underground. It flowed between two and four feet in depth, some of the pools being reinforced by the efforts of beavers. It was my idea of the perfect trout steam, a small but rocky Barle, its surface pitted with eddies, turning, twisting and gurgling its way into its hole in the ground. I confess that a small edge was taken off my enjoyment by the previous night's chatter about rattlesnakes, but I never saw or heard one. By half past eight the next morning, after a disturbed night (I fancied that we were being invaded by mountain lions) and after a mass of eggs, crispy streaky bacon, pancakes, toast and coffee, all cooked on the portable propane stoves we had brought with us, we set out in search of sport.

The sun was high and the water, to my growing excitement, was covered with hatches of small flies, which the fish were sipping fearlessly. Though they were wild trout living in a food filled stream and though, as it turned out, they had learned to avoid flat fish and plugs, they had never, I think, been offered anything that was a close imitation of the natural. By lunch time I had caught eight sizeable rainbow and brown trout, pound sized and very exciting indeed, on 5x gut. I had been broken once and had put back five. I could not remember a fishing morning, in bright sunshine, like it. It needed a great deal of self-effacing modesty to avoid becoming hated by the other four fishermen whose total catch was not quite half mine. They had discovered, too late, that American mountain trout prefer almost invisible English flies. As the Wild Turkey flowed – lethal stuff too, because it tastes so good and is 100° proof – I handed out the addresses where the magic insects could be bought. I later heard that substantial orders were received in Hampshire from addresses in Nebraska, Wyoming and Idaho. 'Do they consider you a good fisherman over there, Dave?' (the U.K. was always referred to that way). It was not easy to answer with tact; the truth would have sounded insulting. 'It's hard to be sure of these things', I replied 'but I'm told that I am one of the top ten dry-fly fishermen in England.' This bubble reputation followed me into other parts of the Middle West on later visits. It also pushed me down a wrong track. For many years I would say to the world at large that, lovely people as Americans usually are, talented and generous to a fault, they have this one shortcoming. None of them can fish.

It took a holiday at Henry's Fork of the Snake River in Idaho to teach me how wrong I have been and how subtle, talented and sophisticated the best ones are. Now I send to Henry's Fork Anglers Inc for some of my dry flies.

Before we returned to the USA, many years later, for the very serious and unsurpassed rainbow trout fishing in Idaho, we had a short, but emotional dalliance with Ireland. One summer my sister-in-law came over. She and Marjorie abandoned me for a five day trip there. We very seldom abandon each other. When 'they' are away I drift somewhere and fish, or stumble around home like a gargoyle, eating little (in spite of the treasures they will have left in the refrigerator), drinking too much and feeling close to a martyr's sainthood.

They came back with fishing news. Down in the south-west the country was beautiful and the rivers were full of salmon and seatrout. Like most Irish reports this was a gross exaggeration, but my curiosity was stirred. I was growing more adaptable every day, and more able to face the difficulties and privations of foreign parts. One day in December I read an advertisement in the *Sunday Times*. It told of brilliantly cooked food and salmon rivers – the catch delivered, smoked within twenty-four hours – and marvellous company. This was one of the inspired productions of Ernie Evans, the master of the Towers Hotel at Glenbeigh. I had a rapturous reply: 'The fish are so plentiful you can walk across the rivers on their backs – and every night we have gay parties.' There was no stopping Marjorie. I was beginning to get afraid that she might even discover (like so many Americans) an Irish family connection. After all her mother's name was Doughty.

We fell quickly under the spell of Ernie and his hotel. A great unwieldy man with Kerry's milk chocolate accent and a smile in every syllable, plus the downbeat sense of humour and fun that so many Irish have. He was the kind of host whose company you cherish. The place was packed. The Clancy brothers were there on holiday, but not singing. Françoise Sagan was there with a group from France, but would not come fishing with me. The night hours were sung away by us all, getting more sentimental by the minute. In the background a pianist treated us to unending ragtime streams of Scott Joplin. Not until about 2 o'clock was there much hope of sneaking off for a bit of a rest.

Overseeing much of this was a delightful receptionist, Mary, who effortlessly convinced every man that in him she had met her fate. 'David', she said one evening as we danced, 'I think you must be the most attractive man in the hotel.' I whispered this in triumph to Marjorie a few minutes later. She shook with laughter. 'I've just heard her telling someone else the same thing.'

We fished two rivers, the Caragh and the Laune. Though we never saw fish in the promised numbers, we had some successes. The Caragh ran a mile from Lough Caragh into the sea, by way of a famous sea pool which sometimes seethed with fish. We flogged it at every chance, but only once did anything take my fly. It turned out to be a three pound mullet, the only one I have ever caught.

The Laune, altogether a much longer river, flowing out of Lake Killarney, ends up in the estuary at Killorglin. I caught fish in both the hotel's stretches. The more interesting was the Beaufort beat, where for some misguided reason of invisibility, huge broad hedges had been cultivated along the banks, over which you fished. It was like casting over a series of low haystacks. There were gaps in the hedges through which the fish were landed – all very well if you had a gillie, which I did not. The fishing was close enough to the sea to give every chance of a fresh fish and in a small flood one day, I hooked one of these. It was like a tiger, ripping off line, splashing and jumping, but the hook held (I was using single hooks in those days and have that particular one still stuck in a sweater all these years later). Eventually I found myself holding it in the current, across this enormous hedge. With the adrenalin flowing like blood and, having no net or gaff, I slipped into the water in one of the gaps in the hedge. I gasped as the cold Laune rose to my armpits, filling my waders, before I touched bottom. Grabbing the played-out salmon by the tail (it weighed eleven pounds) and manoeuvering it, myself and my rod out of the depths and up the bank was one of my most creditable pieces of fishing ever. I was in my forties at the time. I would not even try it now – or I doubt if I would. Just behind me where this happened, up a high bank, was something I had never seen before – a small lawn that was dazzling blue with gentians growing out of the grass.

We had some fine bright holidays at the Towers. It was mostly possible to take time off for other excitements – golf at the wild and ancient Dooks course, or even the Cahirciveen Races held round the Kerry coast on a course that embraced half a mile of sandy seashore. They were running late the afternoon we went and the announcer had to shout, 'For God's sake get them started; the tide's coming in'.

We finally parted with Ernie Evans because he started to charge a proper price for all that he provided – and it was more than we could afford. The place filled up with rich Germans; and much credit to their good taste. Ernie's food was as near perfect as food can be. We had not been able to help seeing, most nights, pale and bitter-looking men in serge suits, sitting among us. 'Take no notice of them', we were told. 'They are the black Irish.' The troubles had begun again. 'F . . . off English' was written on walls and bridges. We departed with very mixed feelings and a hangover so immense that I had to stop a dairycart on the way back to Cork and beg a pint of live-saving milk.

CHAPTER FIFTEEN

The Norman Conquest

During those first July days at Craigellachie, we were very much aware of a table of French; French fishermen, French husbands, French wives. They vanished, we all thought, far too soon. They came in to an early breakfast, full of action and handshaking and laughter. They were gone from the hotel by half past eight, taking packed lunches with them; they came back to high tea (when we were in our baths and gritting our teeth in preparation for the hardship of meeting in the bar), and were off again for the full session of evening fishing. They had all made the decision to put fishing first – something which we did not always do; the temptations of evening drinks and a long wine-laced dinner usually prevailed – though some of us struggled down to the river again later, if we could put on our waders without struggling. We all agreed that they spoke the most perfect-sounding French. We later learned that most of them also spoke perfect English.

One evening (when some of them were not fishing late, as the river was in spate) a very attractive French lady (whom every man in the party had contemplated with admiration) spoke to me as we were getting our coffee in the lounge. They had heard that we were having a desperate week. Their own score on Carron and Laggan was in the twenties. 'You will fish with me and Jacques, tomorrow evening?' she asked. My eyes glazed. People simply do not ask complete, or almost complete, strangers to their fishing; they are rarely that generous. Yet during the week that followed, and in the years that also followed, we were all invited, in turn, to an evening on Carron. It meant, of course, that they themselves had to refrain from fishing, the rods being specifically limited. The French became and have remained, our new very best friends.

I will not forget, in a hurry, my first evening. At the bottom of the beat is the very famous, admired and well-loved pool, Delchapel. You wander down to it from Laggan House, across a meadow and over a stile – and there it is, a long pool out of which the water eventually pours from a wide V into the top pool of the beat below. When the river is high, that top pool looks like a maelstrom. Jacques was going to be my guide and gillie. After inspecting my fly and finding it satisfactory, he told me in slow impeccable English, that it would be necessary for us to go more than half way across. 'It is fast', he said, 'but there are no big rocks'. The fish lay along the other bank and had to be fished from above. I had got about a third of the way over when I felt my wading staff start to vibrate. The water was pressing on me as it roared by. I halted. I had no inclination to go further. 'More Mr. Barr, further over please.' Jacques was walking upstream of me, rod in one hand, no wading stick. He might have been strolling on a well-cut lawn. Each step across that I made myself take increased the pressures. My mouth was dry. If England's honour was at stake, I was ready to abandon it. 'There's nothing to fear', Jacques shouted above the roar of the water, 'there are no big rocks.' Another yard and I was literally hanging on by my toes, stiff with fright. 'Two more paces and it will be better.' I could see my floating body heading toward the rocks and the next beat below. Somehow, beyond the point of no return, I edged on and felt the pressure drop. It took my few remaining shreds of courage to stand upright and start casting. I had never before prayed not to get a take – but inevitably, five minutes later, I was into a fish. 'Move back to the bank gently, Mr. Barr.' Jacques was delighted – which was more than I was. I do not remember the return journey. Playing the fish must have taken my mind off the perils and I ended up with a six-pound grilse. 'We will go and get another?' Jacques asked. I had to admit that any courage I once had, had drained from me. 'We will go to the Bridge Pool then', he said with a smile, 'it is more easy there.' My place was taken by Jacques Montupet, one of the organisers of the fishing (and later to become another real friend). He was delighted to have the chance to fish the pool we were abandoning. Half an hour later Jacques passed me while I fished the serene and gentle tail of Bridge Pool. He had a smile a foot wide and was dragging beside him a salmon that weighed (as I found out later) an ounce or two under twenty pounds. This Jacques (like the other Jacques) had an invariable habit of catching fish; they are all in the top league as fishermen.

Carron is the beat that I associate totally with our French friends. They bring to it each year an air of Gallic excitement and merriment and their pronunciation of the pools – Delchapel, Pol Dornay, Delmonik – gives each one the sound of a lovely place in Normandy, or a grotto in the Cevennes.

During the years that followed, Jack Bridger and I must have spent many evenings as their guests and nearly every time we caught what was often our first fish of the holiday. Much of this was due to the skills of Jacques Tissier, who homed in on taking fish in a way, and in places, that I have never seen surpassed. In a small return we were able to persuade the Tissiers to spend a couple of nights with us on their way home. Jacques fished the Babingley (very appreciatively, 'We have few streams like this in France') as it had never been fished before. With superlative casting in every kind of surroundings, he dry-flied his way from bottom to top, fishing thickets and overgrown stretches that we had never dreamed of attempting – or thought worth the effort. He kept no score but must have caught and returned thirty on his barbless hooks. We, in turn, went abroad – a night at their flat in Paris and a couple of nights at their immeasurably beautiful farmhouse in Normandy, complete with its own cider press and trout stream – and with seatrout fishing within a few miles. They were very happy times with very nice people.

Then one morning, three years ago, there was a letter in my post from Jacques Montupet offering me a rod on Carron as a paying guest – to replace one of the French regulars. This Jacques is a man of many parts. He has a delicate finger in fishing pies all over the world. At Christmas he usually writes to me listing his many successes – not only in Scotland, but also in Labrador, Alaska and anywhere salmon can be caught. He writes in an apologetic, wry style (in perfect colloquial English) which shows that he keeps it all in perspective. I have been trying to tie in the ups and downs of the Stock Exchange with his flying visits, but have not at present proven any link. I did notice that his was the name of the company that took over DeLorian in Northern Ireland.

Just before I went north, on my own this time (and feeling lonely even before I set off), for that first full Carron week (repeated ever since with an extra rod for Alan Blower), Jack Bridger had a devastating stroke. For a year or two he had been ailing, finding it difficult to keep up his usual scale of activity. He was paralysed and unconscious when I left home. The prognosis was very bad indeed.

Two evenings later I was fishing the upstream part of the beat, left bank, just downstream of Millionaires' Corner, when I saw Jacques Tissier walking along the opposite bank. I was at a slow peaceful part of the pool and I could hear his message clearly over the noise of the Spey. 'Some bad news has come for you at the hotel', he shouted. 'Jack Bridger died this morning.' His death, in the extreme circumstances, would have come as a blessing to his loving family. I also know that he would have chuckled to hear it announced in this way. That, and the fact that I was missing Marjorie badly, led to my leaving for a dash home, on the Friday.

Since then, the Carron week has become an annual event

– the highlight of the year's salmon fishing. The team now consists of Alan Blower and me, the Tissiers and two other French friends, Pierre Netter and Gabriel Chambon. Pierre is quiet, twinkling, English speaking and a very good fisherman. On at least one night in the week he will start buying bottles of champagne. 'Please do not worry', he says, 'remember that I am very rich indeed.' Gabriel is what I would call a spirited fisherman – a man of great strength and stamina. He wades everywhere with reckless determination. A week never passes without seeing him and his rod disappear beneath the surface, but he never fails to catch his share of fish.

American Independence Day normally falls during that week. Last year (Pierre's champagne night), we were standing in a group outside the hotel, singing, 'A bas les Anglais', in an inoffensive sort of way, when one of the guests, a captain (whether army, navy or golf-club, I never found out), shouted at us that we were behaving disgracefully and told us to go back to France.

In the July after Jack's death, John Norman took over his rod at Craigellachie. It was the continuation of another long friendship, but the beginning of a new fishing era, during which I have been continuously benefitting from John's know-how and original thinking, and also (with other friends) from the results of his enterprising entreprenurial holiday planning.

He had not fished before with Dick, Alan and myself. We knew he had fished many smaller rivers and had twice represented England in still-water fishing. We were the ones who knew about fishing big rivers – or that is what we thought. We were a tiny bit condescending, considering what a friend he was, and very luckily still is. We raised our eyebrows, delicately, when we saw that he was using a shooting head line; not, we thought, the kind of thing Spey pundits would contemplate. We were going to learn a lot that week.

The Spey's Boat Pool is (as already described) a fine, large-river salmon pool. The current surges into it in a massive diagonal. It ends with a fast run along the far bank, which gradually straightens, then funnels into 300 yards of quick but gentle water, culminating in rapids at the tail of the pool, before a left bend into the beat below. Trees, bushes and sandy bays edge the Boat Pool, and the main taking place, fishing from the right bank, is at the head. To fish it, you edge gingerly into the current, fitting the feet into a pitted bottom, and, standing precariously among the rocks, cast a long line to the opposite bank. With a high background it is not all that easy.

I told John on the Monday morning that I would show him the best way of fishing the Boat Pool. I crunched and staggered my way into the current and round the raging rocks until I had reached a little farther than I had ever before dared to go. I started casting, short ones to begin with, gradually lengthening.

After five minutes' elegant demonstration, my line tightened and the reel began to chatter. I lifted my rod imperiously and was into a fish. I played it as I backed perilously to the bank and soon slid it onto the sandy shore. It was a four pound grilse. I was not to know that it would be my only fish of the week, but, for that moment at least, John was duly impressed. When, on the first day, he had caught nothing, we said to ourselves, 'Not surprising', looking at his tackle. A tiny nondescript fly like a nymph on a double hook was on the tail, a larger one was on the dropper.

The water was half an inch above summer level and we were fishing with a single fly – a larger one than John's dropper, but still, we thought, pretty small. He told us in the bar that he had had three pulls – and from the looks we carefully exchanged, it was clear to us all that the pulls would not have been from salmon – rocks, probably.

It was back to the Boat Pool next morning. As I sat waiting

my turn to fish the run in, I saw that John, who was across from the middle of the pool (an unheard of place to try), was into a fish. Minutes passed and the fish seemed no nearer to being landed. We imagined that John was finding life different from the shallows of Rutland Water. Suddenly he broke into a run, helter-skelter downstream, and we could see his fish splashing fifty yards below him at the tail of the pool. We charged after him and managed to manoeuvre him and his rod across the junction of the Fiddich and onto the right bank of the next beat. We hoped the tenants would raise no objection.

He finally landed it, dead, another 200 yards downstream. It had been hooked in the tail. We felt that someone using a swarm of small flies must expect such misadventures. That evening, at drinks time, he told us that he had had two more pulls and had also lost two fish. We experts, who had fished all day without a touch, listened with polite scepticism.

By the fourth day his total of fish caught had reached five, while the rest of us had amassed beween us one grilse and one seatrout. He had lost a number of other fish and had had all kinds of pulls and tugs. Considering that we had come to believe that the river was empty, he was not doing too badly. It was just beginning to dawn on us that something significant was happening.

We started to spend time buying John drinks and persuading him to tie some of his flies for us. He is not the man to need bribing. He distributed his little lures as quickly as he could create them.

The Norman red-spotted stoat's tail, the tail fly, is tolerably nondescript, except for the tiny red spot. This is the fly that catches fish. The droppers are, in their way, a form of ground bait or eye-catcher. Even so, armed as we became with Norman specials, it was not as easy as we had thought. There was a fishing technique required as well.

Though our catches improved (and a woman fishing the

other half of the beat caught her first-ever fish, a four-pound seatrout, on the magic fly in bright sunshine), we soon realised that the shooting-head line was playing its part. Some of its success was due, in a way I do not understand, to the fact that the cast is straight across (not the customary diagonal), and is followed by a complex series of up and downstream mends. This casting technique is fine with an open bank, but subject to occasional defeat by a close high one.

At the end of the week John had caught seven and lost another six, easily outscoring the totals of the rest of us put together. We had also learned, to our slight shame, that he had fished for salmon for more years, and in a wider variety of rivers, than any of us. It was just his technique that was fresh.

It is worth noting that in 1986 alone, fishing for occasional days on the Torridge, Deveron, Lune, Ullapool, Stinchar and Spey (he has a very fast car indeed), he landed twenty-six salmon and twelve seatrout, all on the big and little fly method. He would be the last to claim that this method is the only one to use – but time and again it brings him success.

As I have said – John's arrival was highly significant for us all and has had many splendid repercussions.

CHAPTER SIXTEEN

West Coast Days and Nights

The Normans, John and June, had been celebrating their summers all over the West Coast of Scotland for years. June felt that nowhere else in Scotland had anything significant to offer; there was not a loch, river, strath, sound or kyle on, or adjacent to, the West Coast that they did not seem to know intimately. When they invited us to join in on one of these adventures, our lives became unexpectedly enriched. We discovered how easy it was to gather together ten or twelve kindred souls and look for mansions to let, in the four figure weekly rental category. This was a leap out of the rut for Marjorie and me, for our holidays had been becoming more and more stereotyped (which is what even a fishing holiday can become if repeated too often at the same time and in the same place. Marjorie never mentioned this, but I now realise that this was how she was thinking). John was, and is, the catalyst and organiser. He is one of those who naturally lead and others follow. A great general was lost in him, but fortunately he has kept his eye on more important things – like fishing. I have never known anyone who fishes so; he is entirely insatiable.

The first of the ventures in which we were concerned together was two weeks at Knock House, a massive mansion owned by Viscount Massarene and Ferrard. The well-furnished house included some of the finest baths (long enough and deep enough to float in, two at a time), some memorable lavatories with mahogany seats and marvellous flushing systems, stags' heads on every inside and outside wall and Mrs. McPhail – the highly talented resident cook who, for two weeks, produced meal of a lifetime after meal of a lifetime. On top of that there were some spacious grounds, peopled by some voracious mosquitoes and biting insects, a resident deer who frightened the lives out of our dogs one night by peering into the car in which they were sleeping, a loch with the appropriate boat and the River Ba running from loch to tidal waters. Thrown in for good measure was the right to fish a stream with an unpronounceable name at the other end of the island, a dozen mildly precipitous miles away.

Fishing, needless to say, was what we had come for. We had sagely filled our guest list with one other rod and a handful of witty, charming, affable and attractive souls, who were happy with whatever else was available and who would have died rather than fish.

There was also a sea-boat – a good thing too, as it turned out. During our fortnight, Mull was the victim of the kind of drought that seems to attack most of my holidays in the North. There were few salmon in the loch – none at all, probably; we never saw one. We soon gave up that fruitless kind of fishing. We caught some small seatrout in two of the Ba's larger pools and one day, hearing of rain in the corner of the island, we set out for our unpronounceable river. There had indeed been a little rain and the trickle had turned into a brook. A bit more rain and it could have been exciting. As it was, we had a pleasant morning and came away with five seatrout, the biggest a pound and a half.

In one of the Ba's two larger pools was a lonely salmon, a big fellow of fifteen pounds or so, which lay in what current there was at the top of the pool and swam downstream into the deep rocks when we disturbed it. We tried every method we could think of – day fishing, night fishing, dry fly, wet fly. Nothing worked until the last night, when walking down to the sea pool, making no attempt at concealment, I flicked a fly over its lie and watched the fish turn and take it. I was so staggered that I struck, as if it were a trout. There was a little tug – and that was the end of it. Some of us never mature.

Everybody took part in the sea fishing. A highly knowledgeable boat driver (a school master when not engaged in this way), took us out into the sound and not only made sure that we had opportunities to catch fish – but also that we got close up views of, and occasionally landed on, the chain of islands. Sitting in a swaying boat with a line in your hand, waiting for some misguided creature to attack the trailed bait, is something that is not the most heart-stopping activity in the world. The mackerel that we caught were so beautiful that it was a shame to kill them – but the blood lust of our non-fishermen and women rose high, so the lovely fish were duly slaughtered and later eaten. I do not hanker for even the freshest best-cooked mackerel. Give me shredded wheat any day.

Great excitement was generated by the lobster pots which we pulled up, emptied, rebaited with some of our mackerel, and returned to re-examine. One day we came back with half a dozen lobsters and a mass of langoustines. That evening, Mrs. McPhail was able to display her brilliance. The plates shone, the glass sparkled, and under the candlelight, on enormous silver salvers, were nests of these marvellous fish, beautifully prepared for easy eating. It was a sight I shall never forget – and a meal we will be lucky to be able to repeat anywhere.

Dry as it was, Mull is an attractive island, a world in miniature – mini-mountains, passes, valleys, little rivers, estuaries, pretty houses sitting tight among the trees and heather. It has so much to offer (and the golf course at Tobermory must never be missed; nor should the bar snacks at the adjoining hotel – a pint of prawns a head) that each one of us went on our way at the end of the fortnight feeling we had had the holiday of a lifetime.

The following year it was Uig Lodge on the Isle of Lewis. Twelve of us again, this time including four fishermen. John had discovered that with this lodge went the tiny River Fhorsa, the usual loch, out of which it flowed, and the sea loch through which it made its way to the sea. The crowning glory of this fishing was the Bruton Run, a 600-yard long stretch where, as the tide dropped to reveal the shape of the river, salmon were to be caught in the brackish water, on the fly.

Although I was just beginning to regard John's information and intelligence sources as without parallel, I was decidedly sceptical about this one. Tidal water? Fly fishing among the kelp? It made no sense – but I would have been happy to rely, in extremis, on the non-tidal parts of the Fhorsa and, of course, the loch. I have never caught a salmon in a loch – but by now the odds must surely be beginning to run in my favour. I am also appallingly incompetent in a boat – regularly getting in the way of the oarsman and, worse crime of all, managing ceaselessly to get hooked to the boat's underside.

The Uig Lodge lettings begin at midday on Saturday. No fishing and no sport on Sunday, of course, but on Monday the week moves into full swing. Marjorie and I, with one or two people to see, made no great effort to get there early. Lunchtime on Monday, or soon after, would be fine it seemed to us. We had a peaceful night in Ullapool and a lovely smooth trip the next morning across to Stornoway. Car unloaded, we made our way across to Uig Lodge.

Lewis roads are not broad, nor straight. Through flat barren countryside, a bit like Orkney, we made our way, crossing occasional streams or small rivers. One – not so small – was the Grimersta (pronounced Grimsta). It did not look much from the road, but is one of the most prolific and exclusive salmon rivers in the West. We averaged nearly thirty miles an hour until we met the marker we had been told about, a single petrol pump and a caravan labelled 'The Stores'. From there it was only a mile or two to Uig Lodge, upright and stark like a small castle in a John Buchan novel, overlooking sea and silver sands.

'Better go and have a look in the kitchen', John said, as we unloaded a ton of gear. I thought that he wanted me to take a look at the highly attractive Cordon Bleu cook we had hired for our week. Not a bit of it. Lying on the board by the sink, were four of the most beautiful small salmon – six to eight pounds – I had ever seen. They were John's morning catch. I never slept a wink that night – in case I missed the next tide.

The Bruton Run that year was a miracle. We were blessed by having the help of Peter Whittingham, one of the nicest and most perceptive of gillies. He knew, almost to the minute, when the tidal fishing should start, and under his instructions we parked our cars, walked along the cliffs each tide, and down into the bay, timing our arrival to the minute. We could already see fish jumping in the distance to our left and, as the tide raced out, we were left with fifty yards of water – diminishing all the time, to cast into. Using single handed rods we worked our size 8 flies into the tide race. Peter stood behind us spotting fish. 'Straight ahead David, quick', – or, 'By your feet, John.' These Hebridean salmon fought like mad-cats. I hooked one that made me run 400 yards down the bay to keep up with it. Peter said, 'He must be foul hooked'; but when I finally wrenched him back from the sea he had so nearly returned to, we found he was hooked in the scissors and weighed only seven pounds. We forgot the river, we forgot the loch, we moulded our lives to the magic moments that came with the tide; an hour and a half's fishing twice in each twenty-four hours. For some of the late sessions I, at least, was too tired to appear – and curiously the night fishing was unproductive. At the end of a week's unforgettable – and unrepeatable – fishing our total was twenty-four fish from the tide. John's 3-0 lead had been whittled down to a narrow 7-6 victory, but as we all know, fishing is never competitive.

We returned the next year, same week, same group of people. We were breathless with excitement. This time we were all there on the Sunday. John Norman would not get three up again. We played a little golf round the lodge on the Sunday – and received a major rebuke for such activity on the Sabbath. Peter Whittingham had gone, but even he could have made no difference. All that week we never saw a fish. The magic had vanished from the Bruton Run. Whatever combination of tide and stream had prevailed the previous year was completely absent.

For our return journey (Uig to Cambridgeshire in a day is impossible) we had booked beds at the hotel at Dalwhinnie. I had asked them for ample deep freeze facilities. They are very obliging people, used to the idiosyncracies of fishermen. They had to make special arrangements to keep their freezers free for, 'upwards of fifteen salmon'. When we arrived with one single salmon, caught in the loch on a dapper, our faces were red.

After that we made two journeys to the lodge at Ullapool, with fishing on the Ullapool River and in Loch Achall. Not long previously, John had fished there and caught nine fish in two days, but the river was in spate at the time. Both times when we were there it was too low to be seriously fishable. There were salmon visible, but they were salmon, which, in those conditions, were invincible. It is an extraordinary river, full of deep pools and rocky bays, and almost alpine climbs. From what seemed like the clouds we could look down and see rows of salmon in the pool called Ness. Climbing down to them was such agony that I stopped going there. It is a secret hidden river and, as such, at the mercy of poachers. To combat these, there is an intricate system of barbed wire entanglements and locked gates. It is, necessarily, a kind of Colditz among salmon rivers. Needless to say, John, in the first year, caught a fish in Loch Achall on his dapping rod – but that was our only success.

We are, nevertheless, thinking of returning. Our lodge is delightful, overlooking the loch. From the bedrooms it is possible to look down its length through one set of windows, and its breadth via the mirrors in the wardrobes. Our holidays were, on both occasions, made enjoyable by the John Norman cook-supply service. The second one was out of this world. She came armed with all kinds of beef, lamb, pork and other good things and, neatly, without fuss and with great sensitivity, she provided us with feast after feast. With enough people to share these pleasures, holidays such as these are far cheaper – and much better – than can be enjoyed in most hotels. If we go again to this beautiful corner of Scotland, we are optimistic that Sod's Law will be reversed and that we will find ourselves with good fishing as well as everything else.

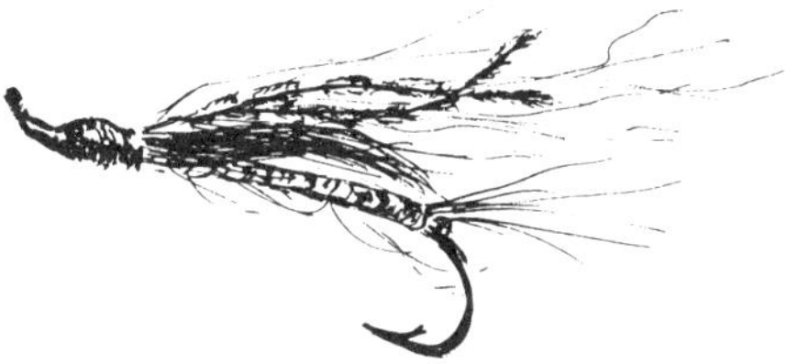

CHAPTER SEVENTEEN

Idaho

Up river, the Snake flows in two sections. One I have never seen, the other is called Henry's Fork. I have never been told who Henry was, but it was in his fork that we did the fishing. Much of its water comes from a gushing spring which forms a small, ice-clear, bubbling pool, filled with enormous trout; it is a tourist visiting place and the fish have an easy life growing large on sandwiches, beef and ravioli. They are tame and friendly. Recently a fisherman who had scattered a fortune over the West in fruitless search for specimen fish, threw senses to the winds and, using bread pellets, caught two, seven pounds each. He was arrested before he really filled his sack but said later, after the trial, that the fine cost him no more than another two weeks' fishing and that having caught two real lunkers he was turning to other sports.

Some miles downstream, below Box Canyon (a fantastic piece of white water fishing), come several miles of the river, converted by the sudden flat lands into serene dry fly water, with underground gardens of slowly waving weed, fierce little watertop eddies, western cattle grazing on the edges, distant frowning mountains – a monster Test transplanted into the golden Idaho countryside. This is the Harriman's Ranch fishing, available to anyone with a state licence and prolific for everyone who overcomes the difficulties of crystal clear water and highly sophisticated wild fish.

Ed Zern (to drop a magic name) guided us to this haven and put us in touch with Mike Lawson (nicknamed The Outfitter). From the picturesque hamlet of Last Chance he runs a tackle and sporting gear shop (that put me in mind of a rustic Hardy Brothers' store), linked to a guide service covering all the magnificent fishing in the area, of which the Harriman's fishing was only a small part.

Marjorie and I were on one of our visits to Scottsbluff, Nebraska, but this time we had made an escape. I had at last become an intrepid birdman and, with hardly a missed heart-beat (she is nerveless), bravely flew in a smallish plane from Scottsbluff to Denver, in a large plane from Denver to Salt Lake City, and in a tiny plane to Idaho Falls. The tiny plane was so tiny that I kept very still indeed, in case I upset the trim, and quietly cursed the other passengers for their reckless movements.

We were met at Idaho Falls by a stunningly attractive lady who turned out to be Mike's wife, Shiralee. All the people we met on this adventure turned out to be Born Again Christians; not drinking; not smoking; very, very careful with their language. On the evidence we saw, it is not a bad thing to be, but we made no effort to join. We were taken in a Japanese-type land rover to Elk Creek Ranch, where we were installed in a genuine log cabin, in which a born again character had lit an enormous log fire. It was September and the nights at this altitude were already frosty. There was a film of ice on the black waters of the lake that surrounded the camp, over which several species of water birds were apparently learning to skate.

By ten o'clock the next morning (all kinds of American tastes for breakfast, American coffee and eggs and bacon, American pancakes soaked in American syrup) the sun was warm and we were on our way back to Last Chance with The Outfitter himself, a signal honour for the English visitor.

That week contained days on all kinds of fishing, including ten-mile float trips (casting as we drifted) down Henry's Fork (with some hairy rapids to survive), and down the beautiful and more serene Madison River (a large, wide Itchen as compared to Henry's Fork), and even a day on the Yellowstone River catching cut-throat trout, beautiful fish of two pounds and more, that found it difficult to resist a sunken nymph – and which fought less well than chubb. During the whole week, incidentally, everything was landed on barbless hooks and returned to the water.

The two days on Harriman's Ranch were outstandingly the finest, two of the kind that get classified as Best in a Lifetime, yet two of the most terrifying – because failure and disaster threatened at all the high moments.

Any ideas of dear old simple, up-stream, dry-fly fishing were quickly dispersed. Rising fish vanished if the trace or leader passed over them, however delicate the cast. At home, a fish taking a three-course meal out of a hatch of flies tends to lose much of his wariness. In Idaho the fish fed even more freely during a hatch, but they never lost sight of the possibility of hidden traps. The fact that some of the fish had been caught several times did not help. It was not an experience that they had enjoyed and the huge head of wild fish (no stocking here), that the river fed and supported, had a sensational growth rate and uncanny brain power.

What I had to perfect was the cast that all the Harriman's fishing experts, except me, made effortlessly – the reach cast. It had been realised that if the fish are frightened by the upstream cast, it was necessary to float a fly downstream over them, the fly floating ahead of the nylon. Without the reach cast, the fly (floating like a little sail boat under its annointment with Gink) skitters across the surface and the fish depart in the direction of Idaho Falls. Drag is the unforgiveable sin.

The reach cast is made fifteen yards upstream of the rising fish. As the fly is about to alight it is pulled gently towards the rod and is then allowed to land, with a loop of floating line that will form and cushion the fly against drag. The fisherman pays further line into the loop as the fly floats downstream, into those open mouths. A really good reach caster can achieve in this way a float, without drag and in the fastest of currents, of up to fifteen yards. At the risk of becoming instructional (in the way beloved by so many book publishers) it will now be seen that you must first locate a rising (or working, as it is called over there) fish; next you must get within range of it without scaring it; next you cast, from above, upstream of it and beyond it – after which the reach cast brings the fly into the correct line – and down over the target it will float.

With eyes like the eyes of the ospreys that circled over us much of the time, Mike allowed our boat to drift slowly downstream – until suddenly, the anchor would be dropped. He whispered, 'There is a huge one working by the bank'. After a while I succeeded in spotting the movements of a big fish, rising easily and regularly – a mound of water rolling with each movement, the slow head and tailer that a salmon will sometimes demonstrate. We lowered ourselves from the boat and waded, up to our waists, towards the fish. Getting into position took all of five minutes, accompanied by interjections like, 'Just look at that tail', and, 'It must be thirty inches long'. Finally he said 'Go get it!' Heart in mouth I cast and the tension played havoc with my amateur reach cast. The fly dropped on the water as if it were a bee and the drag looked like a mouse swimming. That, of course, was that. I could feel Mike's disappointment and his difficulty in concealing his mild contempt. He had always known that those who write so confidently about fishing are poor operators.

By the end of the first day I had destroyed my chances several times and caught nothing. My morale was at a very low ebb. 5,000 miles is a long journey to make a fool of yourself. It was mid afternoon of the second day when I broke the spell. A mile from where we had started I tackled yet another working trout, got in a good cast and float, watched a little hole in the water through which my fly disappeared, struck, and four or five minutes later, very exciting tense ones too, remembering all the time that smooth barbless hook, brought a beautiful rainbow to my side. Mike, standing by and throwing out some born-again prayers, gently cradled it in his hands (not easy to do) measured it, slipped out the hook and lowered it back into the river. It was nineteen inches long, weighed about three pounds and had fought like a seatrout.

It was a magic week in beautiful Idaho. We found time to explore parts of Yellowstone Park, where Marjorie had spent camp-fire girl holidays; to smell the perfume of the real high mountain air, passed through warm pine trees; to spend evenings in long earnest Bourbon-scented conversations with fellow tourists and the locals. She even found herself a horse and helped round-up some of the Harriman's cattle. I could see her from my boat, looking thirty and making the kind of yippee noises they make in Western films. At one time, she told me, there were three different kinds of eagle circling over her.

We were so besotted with Idaho that two years later we returned, this time with William, Erica and their two children, Tom and Helen. Once again the magic worked. Sharing the log cabin we had used the first time, we could enjoy it as well, seen through eleven-year old eyes, eating food that they had never eaten before, seeing birds and beasts that they had only read about. Fishing Box Canyon one day, we had a family picnic and were visited by a strange tame little animal, a rock chuck that was a close relative of a ground hog – a highly enlightening moment as Marjorie and I had been, a little whimsically, celebrating at home, Ground Hog Day, for many years, to the mild perplexity of the Island Race.

As for the fishing, William found it as gripping as he had expected. On the downstream floats he was invincible, working his leaded nymphs into impossible lies and pulling out fish after fish. Wading Box Canyon he could not go wrong, reaching places that were unattainable to me, balancing on the slippery rocks and in the speeding water, impeccable and effortless. Age and plenty to drink the night before showed me up badly. Without a wading staff I was a craven liability, as much use as a beginner on an ice rink. At Harriman's however, class began to tell. My longer experience of the reach cast got me (as they said) to first base, while Will struggled as I had on the previous occasion. On one magic morning, two reach casts that turned out to be perfect produced me fish of twenty-three and twenty-one inches. Whatever more could be found anywhere? Even The Outfitter was impressed. Perhaps a writer could fish after all. Will and his family are sure, of course, to return.

The flies we used were of Mike's own patterns, made to imitate the continuing hatches that illuminated the warm parts each day. They were categorised as May flies – but were nothing like the large British insects of that name. They were tiny, a little like Pale Watery Duns or Pale Olives or Driffield Duns. I brought home a box full and they operate most successfully on almost any dry fly water – all size 14, if I may be forgiven for introducing a thoroughly technical note.

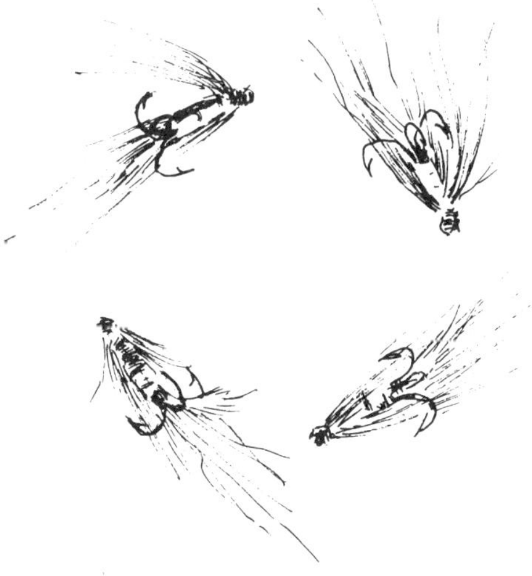

CHAPTER EIGHTEEN

Home Again

Though I am not exactly sure to whom I owe it, my gratitude for a marvellous life is intense and unqualified. If things depend on what is, and what is not, deserved, I have had a highly generous ration of the undeserved.

First of all Marjorie (or Marje as she is mainly called). First and last. If I am good natured, active, creative and in any way unselfish, it is entirely due to her effect upon me – coming up to forty-four years of it as I write. Every good thing that has come my way she has nourished and encouraged – and with a host of friends like we have, you cannot record such things if they are not recognised to be accurate. She is the unobtrusive power house that has turned possibility into certainty. To spend a lifetime with someone who modestly excels at everything, who has brought up the happiest of families, while dominating a career that involved (very often) the rationing of every waking moment, is something that makes the word admiration seem lightweight. I will not forget, when she retired, the letter in the local paper, from one of the big firms of Kings Lynn practitioners, recording the practice's thanks for all she had provided for them at the hospital – adding the obvious, that she was a rare and irreplaceable person. She has also, I should add, a somewhat wicked and very infectious sense of humour.

With her behind and beside me (we still call her plural in the family, all of us do. 'I don't know what they might think of that idea', we mutter) – everything else has fitted into place. The hardest, vilest legal day slips from the mind in the evening welcome to such a home. Disasters are put into perspective; the small gains can become triumphs, pomposities a sudden source of fun. I began to discover that being a lawyer was not an exercise in legal semantics, but a job in which real daily pleasures and rewards were to be found. So complex is the pattern of our two lives' involvement with each other, it would take a thousand pages and far, far better writers than I to give any fine description of what has grown between us.

Next came the writing. I am the third generation of my family who has sold, on a regular basis, the products of his pen. Already both our sons have written published books. Years and years ago I started to write and sell short articles, as much for an end of day relaxation as anything else. The first published one appeared in *The Field*. It was about East Anglian point-to-points, caused a mild stir and great excitement in my heart. To have this stimulation and get paid £8 was unbelievable. Since then, about thirty of my articles have been printed each year, in all kinds of magazines and newspapers, here and abroad. With the effrontery that is typical of anyone who is prepared to cast his thoughts into the market place, I have kept copies of every one. I have reached 870, more than a million published words. *A Family Way*, locally published, sold out its 2,000 copies; *The Haig Guide to Salmon Fishing* and *The Haig Guide to Trout Fishing* that I edited, and contributed to, are today almost unobtainable. Twenty years ago, almost to the day, I started writing regularly for *Country Life* (thereby becoming, I suspect, the best paid of the fishing writers) and I have been their privileged official fishing correspondent for the last dozen of them.

It would also be folly not to mention *Trout and Salmon*, published by EMAP of Peterborough. They printed the fourth fishing article that I wrote and, since then, have published more than forty others – grossing, I imagine, more words than in this book. I worked through highly respected editors like Ian Wood (who spent too much time thinking how to cut contributors' payments), Jack Thorndyke (one of the very best), the very experienced Roy Eaton, John Wilshaw, and now Sandy Leventon, under whose guidance the title is growing in size scope circulation and quality.

Another word about the little Babingley, a small near-chalk stream that flows beyond Kings Lynn, that I have fished since my first months in the Fens. There is not an eddy, not an idiosyncracy in that mile or so of flowing spring water that I do not know, and hardly a fish whose forebear I cannot remember. Marjorie has a theory that my liberty to go there, the turning off a busy A road into the quiet of the park after a forty-minute drive, the peace as well as the occasional frustration, has kept me and ulcers apart, at the times of highest working pressures and has even helped recuperation on the rare times when I have been ill. I fish it with ten others and hope that over the years we have given back more than we have taken. This seems a good moment to record my gratitude for these pleasures to the family that has treated us so generously.

Finally in a short book such as this, there are inevitable omissions. The Stinchar, for instance, a unique spate river, where John Norman and I had a fast and furious three days. Or the Eden, from which the salmon seem to have vanished – but have been replaced by big plump trout. The Usk, too – such a lovely river – but nearly empty each time I went to it. There are many others on which I have been lucky enough to spend time – the Tow, the Torridge and the Tamar, the lovely and fruitful Laune and last but by no means least, the Tillmouth Park water on the Tweed, in November, surely some of the finest salmon fishing in the world. Life, I am afraid, is just not going to be long enough.

À TRÈS **PETITS PAS**

Les volcans

Directrice de collection : Claire Laurens
Édition simplifiée de *Les Volcans à petits pas,* Actes Sud, 2010
Éditrice : Isabelle Péhourticq assistée de Marine Tasso
Directeur de création : Kamy Pakdel
Directeur artistique : Guillaume Berga
Maquette : Sarah Dugrip

ISBN : 978-2-330-01987-7
Loi 49-956 du 16 juillet 1949 sur les publications destinées à la jeunesse.
Reproduit et achevé d'imprimer en avril 2013 par l'imprimerie Pollina à Luçon - L64378c
pour le compte des éditions ACTES SUD, Le Méjan, Place Nina-Berberova, 13200 Arles
Dépôt légal 1re édition : mai 2013 - Imprimé en France.

Les volcans

FRANÇOIS MICHEL
Illustrations : ROBIN

ACTES SUD
JUNIOR

1

Qu'est-ce qu'un volcan ?

Un volcan est une montagne en forme de cône. Elle se construit éruption après éruption.

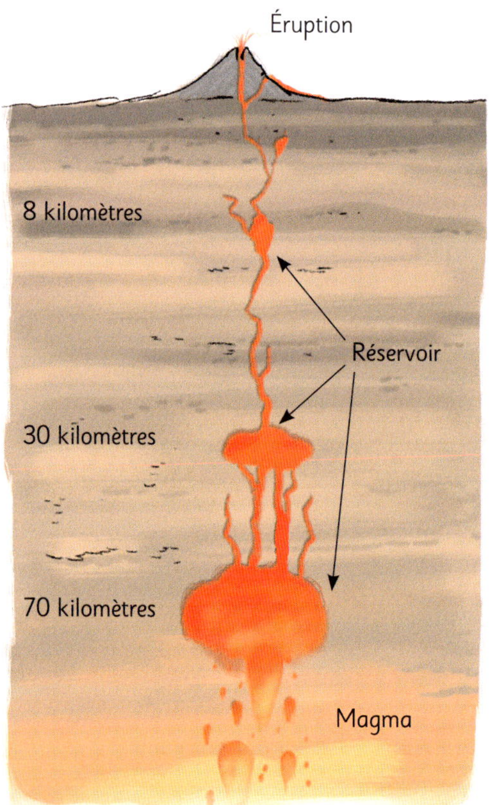

• La partie souterraine

À des kilomètres de profondeur sous la terre, des roches fondent. Elles forment le **magma**. Les gouttes de magma remontent par des **fissures** dans l'écorce terrestre et se regroupent dans des **réservoirs**. Quand le volcan entre en activité, le magma remonte encore et rejoint la surface : c'est le début de l'éruption.

• La partie visible du volcan

Elle se forme à la première éruption. Ensuite, à chaque nouvelle éruption, les coulées de lave s'empilent. Les roches et les débris crachés par le volcan s'accumulent aussi sur ses pentes. Petit à petit, **le cône du volcan grandit**.

LE SAIS-TU ?

Une éruption a lieu quand **la pression des gaz augmente** et fait monter le magma violemment. Il se passe la même chose lorsque tu secoues une bouteille de boisson gazeuse et que le bouchon saute.

2

D'où vient le magma ?

Pour comprendre les volcans, il faut savoir comment est fait l'intérieur de la Terre.

• Le magma, c'est quoi ?

C'est de la roche fondue qui contient des gaz.
Il se forme sous l'action de la chaleur, dans certaines zones de la Terre, à environ 100 kilomètres de profondeur. Mais certains volcans ont une origine encore plus profonde, près du noyau.

• La Terre ressemble à un fruit

Son noyau est très chaud et surtout composé de fer.
Il est dur au centre et liquide à l'extérieur.
Le manteau est plus ou moins solide ou pâteux.
L'écorce terrestre est faite de roches solides.
Son épaisseur peut atteindre 200 kilomètres.

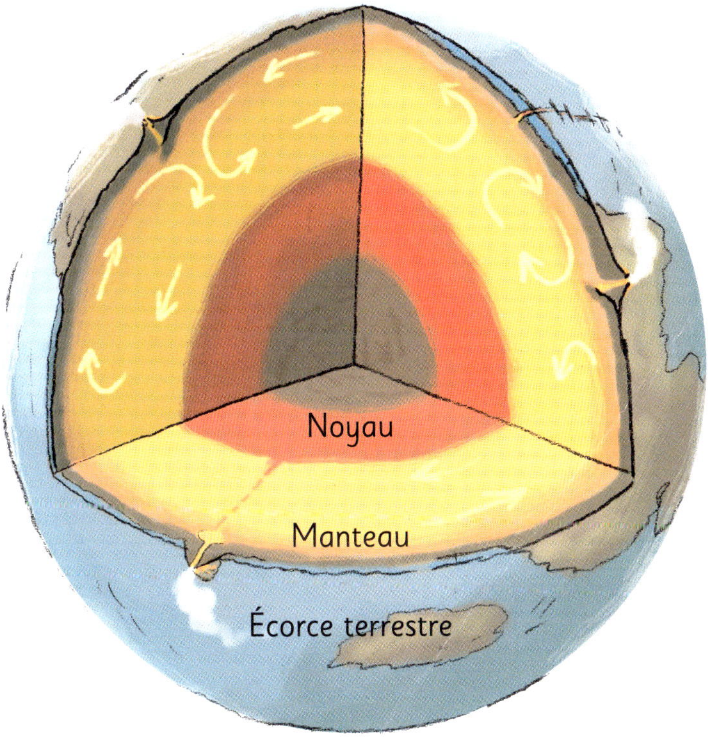

3

Qu'est-ce que la lave ?

Quand le magma arrive en surface, il perd une grande partie des gaz qu'il contenait. Il devient de la lave.

La lave n'a pas toujours le même aspect. Elle peut être **fluide** (liquide) ou très **visqueuse** (épaisse).

• Coulées et fontaines

Une coulée de lave est une rivière de roche fondue qui s'écoule du cratère. Parfois, la lave est projetée en l'air comme l'eau d'une fontaine. Elle peut jaillir à 500 mètres de haut.

• La lave est très chaude

Sa température atteint 1 000 degrés. Les coulées de lave sont dangereuses : elles enflamment la végétation et les habitations. Mais, en général, les habitants ont le temps de fuir.

• Après l'éruption

En refroidissant, la lave se solidifie et devient de la roche volcanique. Si la coulée de lave était très liquide avant de durcir, la surface rocheuse est lisse.

Si elle était épaisse, la surface est plissée ou hérissée de pics qui font mal aux pieds.

4

Un volcan peut-il avoir plusieurs cratères ?

Un volcan est formé d'une cheminée et d'un cratère principal. Il peut en avoir plusieurs.

• La cheminée

Elle s'allonge en même temps que grandit le cône volcanique. C'est le passage principal des laves lors d'une éruption.

• Le cratère

Il se trouve au sommet du volcan. Il correspond au sommet de la cheminée. Quand le volcan est au repos, la cheminée et le cratère sont bouchés.

• Certains volcans possèdent plusieurs cratères

Ceux-ci se forment lors d'éruptions quand la lave s'échappe par d'autres chemins que la cheminée.

5

Toutes les éruptions se ressemblent-elles ?

Les volcans ont plusieurs façons d'entrer en éruption.

L'éruption hawaïenne est silencieuse. La lave liquide s'écoule sur de longues distances et peut même former des fontaines.

L'éruption strombolienne : une lave épaisse sort du volcan. Il projette aussi des pierres et des bombes volcaniques. C'est le cas du Stromboli, en Italie.

L'éruption vulcanienne : le volcan explose brutalement. Il en sort un immense jet de gaz, de cendres et de pierres qu'on appelle une colonne plinienne.

L'éruption péléenne : la lave est si épaisse qu'elle ne peut pas sortir du cratère. Quand le volcan explose, la lave et les roches, volatilisées, forment une avalanche brûlante qui détruit tout sur son passage : la nuée ardente.

ROUGE OU GRIS ?

On appelle volcans rouges les volcans qui connaissent surtout des coulées de lave, et volcans gris ceux qui explosent.

6

C'est quoi, les bombes volcaniques ?

Les volcans qui explosent projettent en l'air des paquets de lave et des roches de toutes les tailles.

Les bombes volcaniques sont des paquets de lave épaisse. Dans l'air, elles refroidissent et prennent différentes formes. Elles peuvent mesurer plusieurs mètres de diamètre et peser plusieurs tonnes.

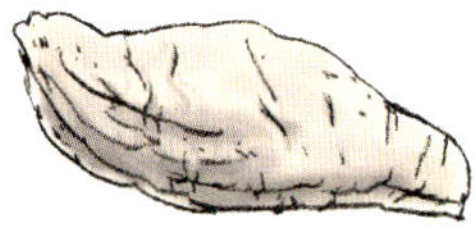

Les blocs sont des morceaux de roche solide. Lors des très fortes explosions, ils sont arrachés au cratère du volcan ou aux parois de sa cheminée.

Les lapilli sont de petites bombes de quelques millimètres à quelques centimètres.

Les cendres sont de fines particules de lave. Elles peuvent monter à plusieurs kilomètres d'altitude et retomber très loin du volcan. Elles forment parfois un nuage si épais qu'il fait nuit en plein jour.

UN FEU D'ARTIFICE

Si une éruption se produit la nuit, on peut voir la trajectoire des pierres brûlantes.

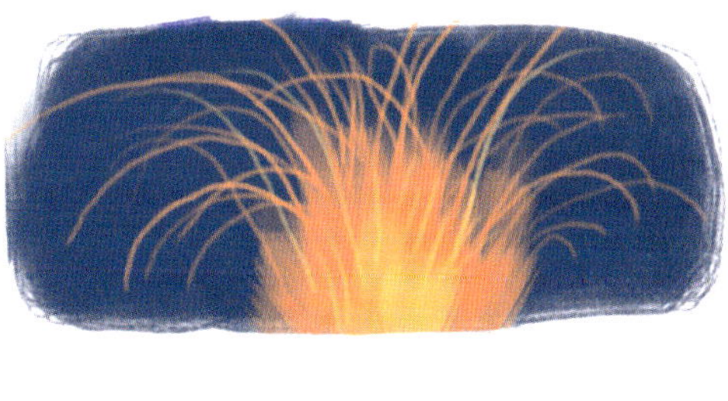

7

Comment se forment les volcans ?

L'écorce terrestre est composée de plaques, comme un puzzle. Les volcans se forment là où elles se rencontrent.

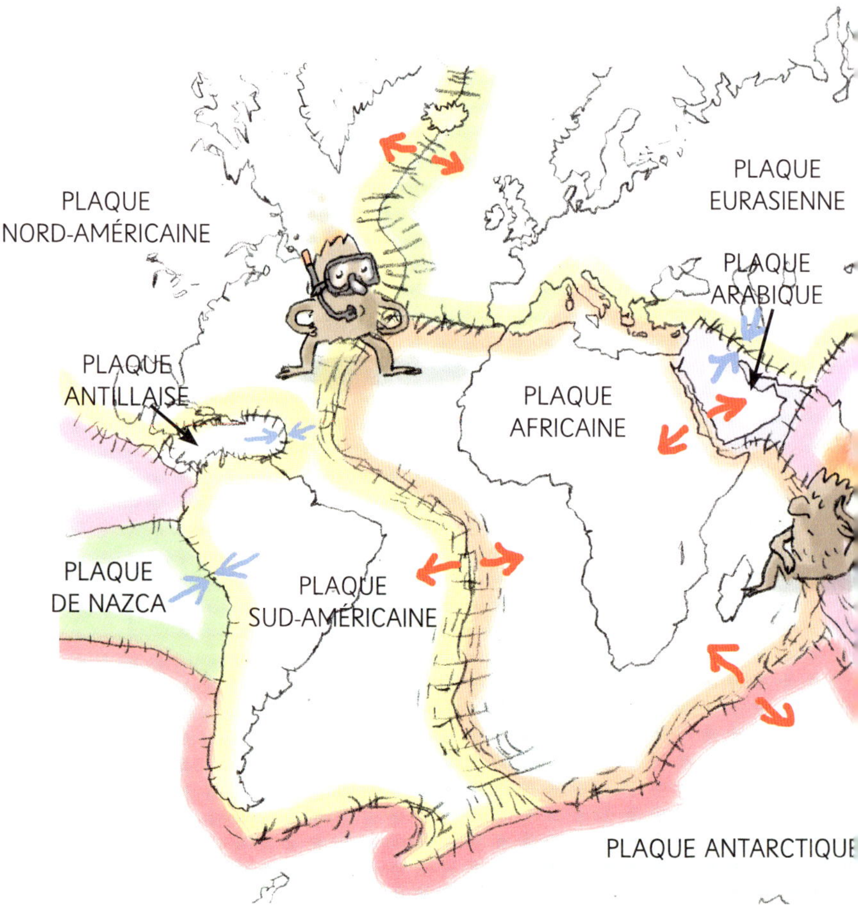

Il y a douze plaques qu'on nomme plaques tectoniques. **Elles se déplacent les unes par rapport aux autres :** elles peuvent s'écarter, se rapprocher, se chevaucher ou entrer en collision. Ces mouvements sont à l'origine des tremblements de terre et des éruptions volcaniques. C'est pourquoi la plupart des volcans se trouvent à la frontière entre deux plaques.

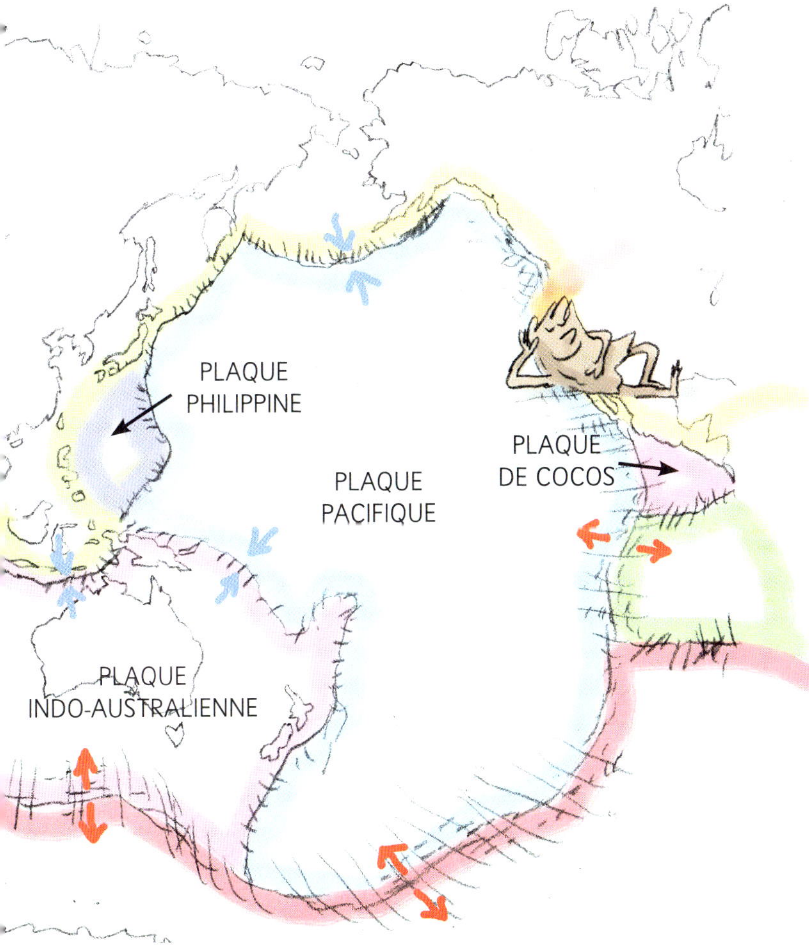

8

Combien y a-t-il de volcans sur terre ?

Plus de 500 volcans sont aujourd'hui en activité dans le monde.

La plupart des volcans se répartissent dans des régions bien délimitées : **la Ceinture de feu du Pacifique**, **l'Indonésie**, **les Antilles**, **la Méditerranée**, **l'Est de l'Afrique** et **l'Atlantique**. Il existe aussi quelques volcans isolés, comme le piton de la Fournaise, dans l'île de la Réunion ou le Kilauea, à Hawaï.

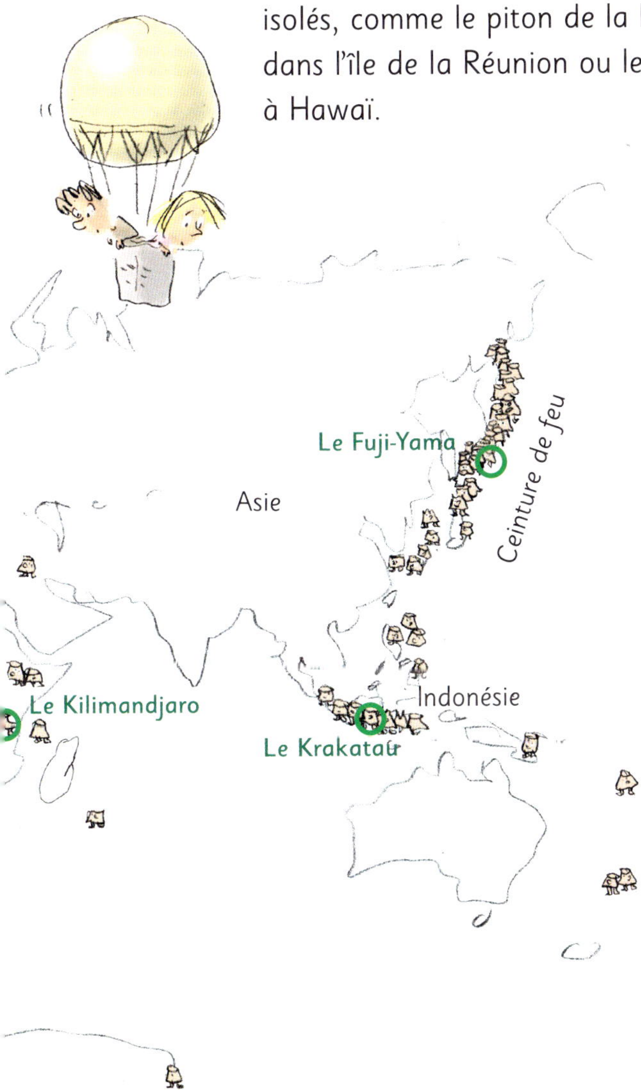

9

Peut-on prévoir une éruption ?

Les volcanologues surveillent les volcans à risque, en y installant des stations d'observation.

• Sous haute surveillance

Des instruments mesurent **la température du sol**, **les séismes** (les tremblements de terre) et **le gonflement des pentes** du volcan. Ces mesures sont transmises automatiquement à un observatoire où des volcanologues les analysent. En cas de danger, ils préviennent les autorités qui décident s'il faut évacuer la population.

• Les volcanologues

Ces scientifiques ne se contentent pas de surveiller les volcans. Ils les étudient pour reconstituer leur histoire et celle de leurs éruptions. C'est la meilleure façon de prévoir leur comportement.

• Bien protégé

Quand le volcanologue fait des prélèvements de lave ou de gaz sur un volcan en éruption, il porte une combinaison spéciale qui le protège de la chaleur, un heaume sur la tête et un masque pour ne pas être intoxiqué par les gaz.

10

Les volcans de France sont-ils éteints ?

En Auvergne, il y a une centaine de volcans. Ils sont endormis depuis longtemps. Mais on ne sait pas s'ils sont éteints.

• La chaîne des Puys

Cette chaîne de volcans se trouve à l'ouest de Clermont-Ferrand. Elle s'étend sur 45 kilomètres. Aujourd'hui, tous ses volcans sont endormis. Mais les hommes préhistoriques les ont sûrement vus en éruption, il y a des milliers d'années.

• Le puy de Dôme

C'est le plus haut et le plus célèbre volcan d'Auvergne. Il culmine à 1 465 mètres. C'est un dôme, c'est-à-dire un volcan sans cratère. Il s'est formé il y a environ 11 000 ans. Non loin de là, le puy de Côme est un volcan en forme de cône. Il se termine par deux cratères emboîtés : le plus petit date de la dernière éruption.

VULCANIA

Au cœur de la chaîne des Puys, ce parc d'attractions te permet de découvrir tout ce qu'il faut savoir sur les volcans.

11

Y a-t-il des volcans sous la mer ?

Plus de la moitié des éruptions volcaniques se passent au fond des océans.

• Des éruptions sans volcan

Sous la mer, il n'y a pas de volcans comme sur la terre. Les éruptions se produisent au milieu des océans, le long des dorsales, des chaînes de montagnes sous-marines. Ces chaînes correspondent aux grandes fractures de l'écorce terrestre.

• Des coussins de lave

Lorsque les laves arrivent au contact de l'eau de mer, elles durcissent et forment des coussins de lave. C'est ainsi que se constituent les fonds océaniques. Chaque année, ils augmentent de quelques centimètres.

• Les fumeurs noirs

Ce sont des sources chaudes sous-marines. Leur température peut dépasser 300 degrés. Lorsqu'elles jaillissent au fond des océans, elles déposent des substances venues de l'intérieur de la terre, construisant des cheminées.

12

Peut-on voir la naissance d'un volcan ?

On a déjà assisté à la naissance d'un volcan : le Paricutin. Il se trouve à 300 kilomètres de Mexico, sur la Ceinture de feu du Pacifique.

L'été de l'année 1942, un paysan et sa femme découvrent **un trou** dans leur champ. C'est un trou très bizarre : ils ont beau y déverser de la terre, il ne se rebouche pas !

En février 1943, en labourant son champ, le paysan entend **des grondements**. Près du trou, s'ouvre une fissure de plusieurs dizaines de mètres de long, par laquelle sortent des cendres.

L'éruption se déclenche. **Douze heures plus tard, le volcan a déjà construit un cône de 10 mètres de haut.** Une semaine plus tard, il mesure plus de 100 mètres. Au bout d'un an, il atteint 300 mètres ! Il culmine aujourd'hui à 424 mètres.

QUIZ

1. Le magma, c'est :

a. de l'eau très chaude

b. de la roche fondue

2. Le magma se forme :

a. dans les profondeurs de la terre

b. dans le cratère du volcan

3. Quand le magma sort du volcan, il devient de la lave.

Vrai

Faux

4. Un volcan peut avoir :

a. un seul cratère

b. plusieurs cratères

5. La température de la lave atteint :

a. 100 degrés

b. 1 000 degrés

6. Un volcan qui explose est :

a. un volcan gris

b. un volcan rouge

7. Les bombes volcaniques sont :

a. des nuages de cendres

b. des gros paquets de lave

8. Les volcans se trouvent le plus souvent :

a. au centre des plaques tectoniques

b. à la frontière des plaques tectoniques

9. Combien y a-t-il de volcans en activité dans le monde ?

a. Plus de 500

b. Plus de 5 000

10. Un volcan peut rester endormi des dizaines de milliers d'années.

Vrai

Faux

11. Un scientifique qui étudie les volcans est :

a. un météorologue

b. un volcanologue

12. En Auvergne, il y a :

a. une dizaine de volcans

b. une centaine de volcans

13. Sous la mer, il y a des volcans en forme de cône.

Vrai

Faux

14. Quelques heures après sa première éruption, le Paricutin mesurait :

a. 1 mètre de haut

b. 10 mètres de haut

Réponses

1 b – 2 a – 3 Vrai – 4 b – 5 b – 6 a – 7 b – 8 b – 9 a – 10 Vrai – 11 b – 12 b – 13 Faux. Il y a des éruptions volcaniques au fond des océans mais elles ne forment pas de cône – 14 b

Tu as allumé
le barbecue
avant de partir ?

DANS LA MÊME COLLECTION :

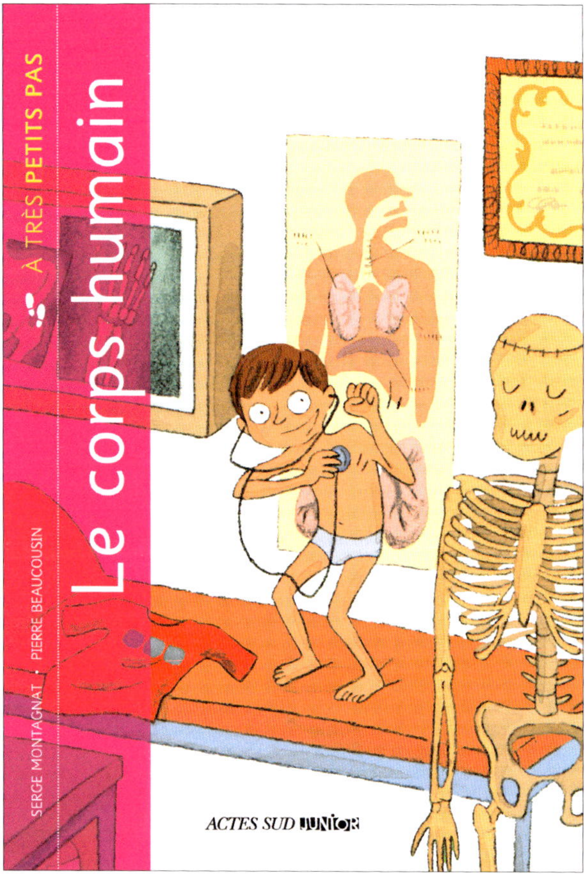

À TRÈS PETITS PAS
Le ciel
MICHÈLE MIRA PONS • ROBERT BARBORINI
ACTES SUD JUNIOR

À TRÈS PETITS PAS
Les aliments
MICHÈLE MIRA PONS • MARION PUECH
ACTES SUD JUNIOR

À TRÈS PETITS PAS
La mer et les océans
GEORGES FETERMAN • GILLES LEROUVILLOIS
ACTES SUD JUNIOR

À TRÈS PETITS PAS
L'écologie
FRANÇOIS MICHEL • MARC BOUTAVANT
ACTES SUD JUNIOR